THE

ART OF TRAVEL BY SOUL

an

Out Of The Body Experience

C. Bert Sanger

Library of Congress Cataloging in Publication Data, 85-61981

POPULAR PUBLICATIONS

P.O. BOX 1558

OROVILLE, WASHINGTON 98844

From the light energy within We form the Holograms of Soul without
To become the light of the world, The Vehicle and the Channel!!

TABLE OF CONTENTS

ACKNOWLEDGEMENTS

The Seattle
Science Center
- For timely display of Holograms which inspired me. La Verna Kashmir, Coordinator. Traveling Exhibits / Science,

Carolyn Sanger
(my wife)
- For allowing me to have the Spiritual space and freedom to write this book, transcribing tapes, typing, etc.,

Donna Mae Nunn
- For inspiration, encouragement, and help in development of the theme of Holograms of Soul,

Mary Hucman
- For providing the image of the motorcycle,

Fred Facklam
- For providing his insight on Truth,

Lois Johnson
- For her support and encouragement,

Evelyn Hedstrom
Mary Ann Hedstrom
- For their continued support,

Columbia Publishing
- For assistance in organization and formatting the manuscript.

INTRODUCTION

My childhood was quite normal as most standards go. I was christened into the Christian Church when I was a child but never felt comfortable with it. My parents and family were loving concerned people and I grew up in the hard work ethic. My father died when I was 10 years old and the great depression of 1930's was well underway. My brother and I grew and sold vegetables for the local market to buy books and clothes for school.

Many of my childhood and adolescent questions were not answered satisfactorily. When I asked about God, Reality, and Truth, I was turned away or put down with "have faith young man" or even worse, "you are not supposed to ask such questions." When people of the cloth, clergy, or ministers who are trained to know such things didn't answer these questions, I soon realized they were embarrassed and actually did not know! My life has been filled with the quest to find the answers myself.

I determined while in my teens that what I needed was to be in the direct path of the Word of God not dependent on the interpretation by another human being who was as fallible as I. If there really was anything to this "God stuff," it had to come from God, not filtered through an intermediary.

Another question that was unanswered was "why do

those people who profess allegiance and loyalty and
even worship of God use His name profanely in the
very next breath they breathe?" This inconsistency
raised questions in my youthful mind as to what God
were we worshipping? I would not be satisfied with
anything less than the Supreme Deity, no lesser God
or Lord would do.

I developed concepts of what I felt and longed
for. These concepts were a fundamental part of my
life long before Sri Paul's writing during the 1960's
and has lasted and increased during the years that
followed.

The fundamental and all encompassing concept
missing within the social religions was that of
SPIRITUAL GROWTH. The path of the Ancient Spiritual
Teaching will guide you to the Truth that will set
you free. The Truth that sets you free is that you
can experience in your imagination, what you desire
to experience in reality, and by maintaining the
experience in your imagination your desire becomes a
reality!

The effort which follows presents a "How To Do It"
type of story. Many of my friends have said they
have read the books or they have completed a study
discourse, but they do not understand its
application. Among my acquaintances there are many
who admit or recognize they do not Travel by Soul
because they DON'T KNOW HOW! To that end, this book
is written. When you, the chela or student, hear it

first hand, how it was done, it is easier to do. The
mechanics of how to do it are stated of many Travel
By Soul experiences by the author who experienced
it. It is an extreme pleasure to be able to share
these many insights of spiritual existence with you
in the hope that you can leap-frog into experiences
of your own.

CHAPTER 1

LEARN TO DISCIPLINE THE MIND

This subject presents a challenge to determine what to say and how to say it. Most of you have read the many books written by Sri Paul Twitchell, who is an excellent writer, and most of you are aware that the living Spiritual Master, Sri Harold Klemp has been trying to guide you on the inner planes. If you have not been able to understand how to Travel by Soul with their help - how can a person like me get the message across to you? I am going to try.

The things I will present to you are those things I have tried and tested; and they work. I will be sharing with you some of the spiritual experiences I have had that have taught me what is going on and what is true. And because of that, I will be using personal possessive pronouns a great deal. It is important to clarify at the start where I am coming from so that you may know I am not on an ego trip. Also, when a personal experience is related, each person who does it will have his own version of it differing from mine. My experience is given as an example of something you might think about and try for yourself.

It would be helpful for you to think of the material as a way of learning how to expand your own spiritual development. I would like to appeal to you to use the questioning approach on everything we do regardless of what you have been doing previously. Just start asking questions because the answers will not come to you unless you ask the question. Do not let your neighbor or your husband or wife ask the question; you have to ask it. There is not a priest or minister or anybody else that will give you the answer. You have to ask _your_ question to get _your_ answer.

As soon as we start any kind of spiritual exercise or process, we are immediately confronted by the mind. Right off the bat the mind is right there. If you are reading something you are using the mind faculty. If you are hearing something, you are using the mind faculty. Everything on this earth plane has to do with the mind. So, I want to start off first by learning to discipline the mind.

When people talk about non-physical things, or they talk about the creation of material things, or they talk about using the imagination, or dreaming or imaging, many people say, "it looks like you are on a big mental trip." This has got to be the great COP-OUT of OUR SPIRITUAL DEVELOPMENT!

A Cop-Out, you know, is an excuse not to do something. It is the reason given for not doing something like Travel by Soul. The person who uses a Cop-Out is a DROP-OUT OF SPIRITUAL LIFE. The one who uses the Cop-Out routine is backing away from the responsibility for the spiritual experience and those things he creates.

You exist where your BEING is. Your BEING is where your consciousness is.

If your consciousness is on another plane - that is where your BEING is. Now, the Great COP-OUT occurs when you ignore your physical body; here on earth, you must be and exist in that body. The mind is part of the physical body and we must work through mind as long as we are physical, or earth bound.

TO REJECT THE FUNCTIONS OF THE MIND IS TO REJECT YOUR EXISTENCE HERE AND NOW! THAT IS SPIRITUAL SUICIDE!!

Rejection of your BEING is the KAL's program! Kal Niranjan is God of the negative planes.

We must work through mind to obtain awareness - whether we like it or not. When we Travel by Soul, we bring back the conscious awareness to our mind or brain. It is absolutely necessary to work out through mind and to return through mind.

We cannot afford to COP-OUT AND TO DO THE KAL'S EVIL WORK!!

We each have different minds; they are each on a different level; they come from different backgrounds. So each of us have the individual problem of disciplining our mind. In order to do that, I would like to demonstrate a dramatic thing. I have in my hand a set of machinist's dies. There is a die for each letter in the alphabet and each numeral. The numerals go from 0 to 9, or from 1 to

3

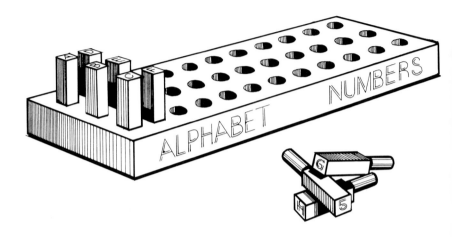

10, whichever you choose. Now, this is the only tool
the mind works with. I would like you to understand
that this is also the whole limitation of the mind -
right here in my hand. There is nothing that the
mind can do that isn't involved with these 36
symbols. We have been thinking that we are great;
that our mind is so great! Mind is a mechanical
organ, just like the heart. It does certain things;
it goes through certain routines every day. Consider
the kidneys which have fluids flowing through them
every day. These organs do not do anything but sit
there (doing their functions). The mind is a bunch
of memories - which makes the mind unique in what it
does. The little computer or calculator in your desk
drawer is activated by the same 36 symbols as the

4

brain. I can hold the set of dies or the computer in the palm of my hand. It is not so great. The mind works the same way; and every time you hear or see or do something, the mind records it on the memory bank and the next time you get the same stimulation, the mind takes it out of memory and recycles the same garbage to the mind awareness. Stimulation is what the computer programmer calls keys or codes to gain access to the memory; and they are developed from these 36 symbols. Other programming symbols are based on the meaning understood in the basic 36 symbols.

We should be aware that we have to do something to get away from the mind. The mind is the thing which controls us in our physical life. It keeps us pushed down into the dirt and the scum and the filth of this physical life. The pure Soul needs something to interpret the physical environment and to allow it to select those things which it needs to survive. So, mind is the filter for Soul, which we should recognize as our true identity.

We are not the physical being we think we are - with these arms and legs - but we are really Soul. In the Christian Bible it is referred to as "man being made in God's likeness." That part of you that is made in God's likeness is Soul. We develop this as our true identity and we recognize each other as Soul; in other words, that part of us which is God-like.

Now, I would like to go a little further with the
mind. I would like to put a diagram up here on this
board so we can start understanding the mind. We
communicate on the earthly plane using symbols,
diagrams and charts. I am going to do the same thing
because that is the only thing we know on this
level. Looking at the Chart 1 (THE SPIRITUAL
WORLDS), we see we are living on the physical plane,
right on the bottom. Above the physical plane is the
Astral plane where you exist without the physical
body. You have another body, or sheath, around you
as Soul. The plane above the Astral is the Causal
plane, next is the Mental plane, with the Etheric
plane between the fourth and fifth planes. The
planes above the fifth plane are the upper spiritual
planes. Each of the religions that I have
experienced worship a god no higher than on the
mental plane - the Christian God, a Jehovah, a Brahma
or whatever you wish to call It. That God is on the
mental plane. That God eulogizes the power of the
mind. Everything is mental; it is a big mental
trip. All of our scientists and the intelligensia
eulogize and praise the mind power. SUPER MIND
POWER. I have been an Aerospace Engineer for thirty
years and was on the team that designed the space
shuttle now making trips into space. I feel that I
know what science and the so-called intellectual
people are doing and where they are coming from.
They are all coming from the mental plane, the fourth

6

Chart 1
The Spiritual Worlds

Name of Plane (LOK)	DESCRIPTION
12. SUPREME DEITY	OCEAN OF LOVE AND MERCY
11. SUPREME DEITY WORLD	ABOVE THE SUPREME DEITY ARE MANY PLANES NOT YET REALIZED
10. ANAMI LOK	NAMELESS PLANE-BEYOND HUMAN LANGUAGE-WE CAN HARDLY SPEAK OF IT
9. AGAM LOK	INACCESSIBLE PLANE-FEW ENTER INTO THIS WORLD-NO WORDS CAN DESCRIBE IT
8. HUKIKAT LOK	HIGHEST STATE SOUL GENERALLY REACHES-SOUL STAYS HERE FOR EONS
7. ALAKH LOK	ENDLESS WORLD-SACH KHAND-ETERNITY SEEMS TO BEGIN AND END HERE-UNKNOWN WORLD
6. ALAYA LOK	INVISIBLE PLANE-SOUL FINDS PEACE AND HAPPINESS-DOES NOT WANT TO LEAVE
5. SOUL	DIVIDING PLANE-FIRST REALM OF THE SUPREME DEITY-PURE SPIRIT-PURE BEING-SELF REALIZATION
----- DIVIDING LINE BETWEEN PSYCHIC & SPIRITUAL -----	
ETHERIC (TOP OF MENTAL)	UNCONSCIOUS-SOURCE OF PRIMITIVE
4. MENTAL	JAHOVAH-SOURCE OF PHILOSOPHY-ETHICS-MORAL TEACHING-AESTHETICS-UNIVERSAL MIND POWER-GOD OF RELIGIONS
3. CAUSAL	KAL NIRANJAN-RULES OVER NEGATIVE REALITY-AFFECTS ALL BELOW
2. ASTRAL	SOURCE OF ALL PSYCHIC PHENOMENA-FLYING SAUCERS-SPIRITS, ETC.-HIGHEST REACHED BY ASTRALPROJECTION
1. PHYSICAL	ILLUSION OF REALITY-MAYA-SCIENCE-PLANE OF MATTER-ENERGY-SPACE-TIME. SOUL TRAPPED BY FIVE PASSIONS: LUST-ANGER-GREED-ATTACHMENT-VANITY.

plane. We now have an interesting situation because
the spiritual planes above the fifth plane are called
the First Grand Division. Those planes below the
fifth plane are called the Second Grand Division. The
Second Grand Division is the creation referred to in
the Bible book of Genesis. This is where we find
ourselves now - on the lowest position of the chart;
the world. Down through all these levels of
existence to earth man in his evolution, or opening
up as a spiritual being, takes on the entity of Soul.
I would like to split the chart up into a "T" in the
Second Grand Division. In this area we have the
co-existence of both mind and Soul. Here on earth we
have a Soul which has to work with mind. We have to
picture this area to understand what we are doing.
See Chart 2. Starting at the top of Chart 2 is the
First Grand Division. These are the God worlds and as
such everything here is real and everything exists.
If something is real, it does exist. So you have to
accept the fact that it all exists up there. In the
Second Grand Division, something interesting
happens. We have a split here between Soul and Mind.
In Soul you have the situation where things are real
and all things exist. Right across this chart in the
mental area, it is all illusion. Those things do not
exist and that is why we have so much trouble. We
are in continual conflict with ourselves. Those
things which mind deals with are distortions,
figments of the mind, information from the memory

8

Planes

	FIRST GRAND DIVISION
12 11 10 9 8 7 6 5	GOD CONSCIOUSNESS - Highest State CREATION IS INCOMPLETE NON-POLARIZED NO CONCEPT OF SPACE OR TIME (INFINITE) ALL THINGS EXIST IN CONSCIOUSNESS CAUSES ALL HAPPENINGS IN SECOND GRAND DIVISION

SECOND GRAND DIVISION

4

SOUL   MIND

3

	AREA OF KNOWING TRUE CONSCIOUSNESS CREATION IS COMPLETE	AREA OF DESIRES STATES OF CONSCIOUSNESS CREATION IS COMPLETE
2	SELF-CONSCIOUSNESS AREA OF REALITY INFINITE EXISTENCE	CONDITIONS AREA OF ILLUSIONS ALL THINGS FIXED IN TIME AND SPACE
1	Soul coexists with mind using mind to interpret sensory environment	CONTINUAL CHANGE

CHART 2

which have been distorted by our karmic stuff; things which are warped out of shape by emotions and the sensory data provided by the five senses - which are all false. None of it is true. When the do-gooders and people who want to solve all the problems of this world talk to you about the big solutions they have, you have to remember that they are on a mental trip and it probably won't work. There is no real solution that I know of on this earth to keep people from fighting with each other. There are millions of minds whose collective consciousness is devoted to destroying each other; messing each other up so that your Soul does not have much chance to be seen or heard or to poke through this maze of illusion that is thrown at it.

We prefer to say, "Hey, this is where I want to be." We say we really are Soul and we want to align ourselves with Soul. Then we can learn what reality is and learn about truth. When we do this we establish conscious states of what we are seeing and doing.

The rest of the picture on the chart shows that those things which are real and true on the Soul side come out as an aberration or unfocused pictures out on the mind side. It is the exact opposite or the mirror image of something, which is an illusion. It is not true at all!

On the mental side, we have to learn to live with the world around us. When a little baby is born, it has to learn all this stuff from its parents. It does not know what is up or which direction is down. It just lies on its back and cries. Its mother has to explain and show it everything, and sometimes it is told correctly and sometimes it is not.

Those things which exist in the Second Grand Division - exist as a state of consciousness. Later in this discussion we will probe into the states of consciousness in depth and learn what they are. We want to end up, before we get through, learning how to travel by Soul or how to have an out-of-body experience. I am trying to share what I know about it and what I have done, to help you get the awareness you will need. You need some tools to work with and some skills to bring it about. I hope that you can get this kind of awareness of Truth because that is where we are headed. This is going to be a real interesting sleigh ride - so grab a hold of your chairs and hold on!

On the earth plane we have the mind to deal with. I asked you previously to develop the ability to ask questions. The whole mind process is based on questioning. So whether you think mind has anything to do with spiritual development or not, take a few moments and try some of this stuff, see if it works for you. You have to doubt in order to gain understanding. It is understanding that we are trying to reach. Understanding is what brings us to self-knowledge. Your knowledge of yourself is the

11

means by which you progress. O.K., now let us get
back to the mind and what it takes to control it. We
said that we have a mind that is running wild and it
works almost entirely on recycled verbiage and
recycled garbage we have experienced in the past. So
we have to do something for the mind to change the
whole situation. We have to provide some kind of a
discipline. The mind works real well with discipline
and there is nothing the mind likes better than a
fire drill. If mind can repeat something over and
over again and put it in its memory bank, it is
happy. That is what the mind process is all about.
     The mind does not think; the mind has no ability
to think at all. It is Soul that provides the
ideas. Never the mind. The mind is like your
heart. The heart just sits there going
thumpity-thump, thumpity-thump; it does not do
anything else. The mind is the same way - it just
regurgitates all the things it has in memory
storage. So - we must provide some discipline. We
must give the mind something to do. As long as we
bump along in our daily lives just letting mind cough
up all its old stuff that is already recorded, it is
not going anywhere. We need to provide some idea,
some code word; like the machinist's dies, in a form
the mind can understand; some message from Soul - now
that sounds like we are zeroing in on our need.
     We exist in our present form as both Soul and
mind; so let us try to get some pure ideas from Soul;

12

some of the beautiful things from Soul; some of the
harmonious things from Soul. Let's try to get the
things that are tranquil, smooth, sweet; and all the
nice things that we enjoy in our lives, and forget
all the rot that the mind keeps throwing up at us.
Then mind would have something solid to work on.
That is where we are right now. We are at the point
where we can get something transferred from Soul to
the mind, and we can live a more pleasant life.
Also, while we are in the physical body - we need to
learn this technique and awareness so that we have
some talents to work with.

It will not happen, friends, if you sit there like
a wart on a pickle and do nothing. That won't cut
it! Even if you are a member of an Ancient Spiritual
Teaching, but you do not learn what you have been
sent here to learn, you won't cut it. You have to do
something for yourself. You have to start moving and
developing yourself. We really want to put Soul in
charge of our lives. If we could get Soul to take
charge once a week, as when you were following a
religion, you went to church once a week; would that
be adequate? How about doing it once a day - or
every hour - or every second? We should try to do it
every second. Then we can understand what is
happening and maybe we can improve our situation.

In order to do this, let us review our spiritual
exercise technique. When we are on the path of an
Ancient Spiritual Teaching, we are given some

instruction on how to exercise spiritually. Each of
us learns something about having a spiritual
exercise. When you do this type of thing - what do
you do? Some of you go to sleep; some of you snap
out of your sleep with a nice feeling; some of you
don't really know what happened, but you feel good
after it; some of you recall beautiful colors or hear
nice music. Each person seems to have a different
experience because we are individual spiritual Souls.

When you were initiated in an Ancient Spiritual
Teaching you were given a word, a personal word. I
don't know if you use that word or not, or whether it
works for you - if it does work for you that is
fine. If it does not work for you - maybe you should
get another word.

Let us talk about contemplation. If you know what
contemplation is perhaps it can help you in your
spiritual exercise. You are acquainted with how the
Monks go into a little cloistered group far away from
society and pray. The Yogis do things which are
quite popular today as health and physical fitness
exercises. A Yogi will stand in a corner of the room
on his head and say he is comfortable and relaxed.
Or the Yogi will settle on the floor with his legs
wrapped in a lotus position, saying he is relaxed and
free of thought. They expect great truism or
enlightenment to happen to them. This is meditation
and it is very passive in its approach.

The Yogi gets himself into a blank condition

mentally - and that part of it is alright; but if you
sit there passively, waiting, and waiting, you are
going to sit there several minutes. Then the mind
will take over again. The mind cannot sit idle very
long before it churns around with some of its
memories. Mind will seep back into the awareness and
sweep away whatever you have done - destroying it.
The concentration span limits how long you can sit
there. The more active your mind is the more
difficult it is to meditate. Meditation is not
successful because it involves the memory junk the
mind is trying to recycle on you. Since that is just
what we want to get away from - we must say that
meditation won't work for us.

Contemplation is something quite different.
Contemplation says that if we go into the third eye -
between the physical eyes on the forehead; focus the
attention and blank out all mental activities, that
now we are ready to have a spiritual experience. You
become an active participant in what is done. You
bring some ideas over from Soul to give mind
something to work with. This is the principle on
which Travel by Soul is all about.

Travel by Soul makes everything possible; every
wish and desire that you have, everything you might
want to do or see, or think you can experience. It
is possible for you to do those things. I have done
it and I know it works! I would suggest for you now
that you determine this is the time to change.

15

Whatever you were doing before in your exercises, decide to do something different. Do something you think might work. This is a wonderful thing - you can go from one experience to another experience. Contemplation is the way to become an active participant in your experience.

The most important part of mental discipline is the setting of goals. Setting of goals or objectives is good for the mind. The mind likes this kind of stuff. It eats it up! When you set a goal the mind will function enthusiastically. Find something the mind can accept. You could write down what your goal is in the discussion we are having with Travel by Soul - see what your going-in consciousness is. See if you can come up with a reason for why you are here. The goal can be going shopping or any one of a thousand things. You can decide that your mind will accept a spiritual goal. The spiritual goal can be supplied by Soul. Now we are beginning to bridge the gap and get something going.

To master one's life, one must be a Doer of God's will; become the CAUSE in the cause and effect relationship. When we separate ourselves from God as a Doer, we revert back to being a searcher again, or a believer again - both of which are passive. I suggest that you change your spiritual goals from "Seeking God" (beseeching, exploitation, prayer), to that of "Serving God" (the mastership of your everyday affairs).

CHAPTER 2

LEARN TO EXPERIENCE REALITY

Now, we will talk about Reality and learn to experience Reality. What is real - or what is reality? What do you think reality is? Is it listening to the wee small voice within us? That has to be accepted as something real - the intuitive intuition type of thing - maybe? Somehow the mind has retained something that happened in a dream and brought it back to your consciousness maybe that is real? When you have flashes of insight, if one could do something to open up the flash second into something you could repeat or even extend the time duration, you might feel that something had been accomplished.

Developing the flash insight into something is a good starting place and I will share with you what I know of how to use it. When you have a flash insight ... take that experience and analyze yourself to get the self-knowledge of yourself. Ask yourself what happened. What did I do? What was the condition I was in? How did I feel? What was my attitude? Was I warm and comfortable? Was I thinking of anything in particular? What was I trying to accomplish at the time it happened? Was it something that had a build-up in time or over a period of time? What emotions did I have? You can reset the stage and

relive the whole darn flash second again! You can
set yourself up so that it will happen to you again.
Now when you get skilled at this, your whole life can
exist within this beautiful insight - 24 hours a
day! Your Soul is coming through. As long as you
are having problems or hang-ups, your mind is going
to blank everything out and won't hear the wee small
voice. Once in a while there is a little crack or a
seam in your mental operation that allows the insight
to come through.

Each plane has its own reality. Each plane and
all the different levels that your Soul occupies has
its separate reality. We can experience reality on
the mind level and all these five Second Grand
Division Worlds (including the Etheric Plane). We can
experience Soul reality in these lower worlds and the
spiritual worlds above in the First Grand Division of
creation, because Soul exists in all of them. Now,
this is kind of fun for when you go into an
out-of-body or Travel by Soul experience - the Soul
reality is the only reality you are working with -
for the simple reason that you do not have your
physical body along on the trip. You don't have the
physical body's five senses: seeing, smelling,
feeling, hearing, tasting type of things. You have
spiritual senses, those higher senses that give you
this kind of input. So you have all the sense
perception you have now. On each level you will have
a different input in reality.

The thing that we have to remember is that each of the experiences that were real to you is your own personal property. The reality belongs or exists only for you. Nobody else experienced it and it is not real to anybody else. When you have an experience, revel in it; feel great; feel the warm feeling that goes up your spine and whatever it does to turn you on! Let it turn you on; and then try to capture it and expand on it.

We are going to learn how to expand on that experience, because that is what we are here for. I will lead you through an experience.

Will each of you close your eyes; just sit there comfortably. I am going to describe something I want you to do. Picture yourself in the living room of your home. If you are reading this material in your living room, then picture yourself in the home of your parents or that of a friend. You are in the living room sitting on the couch or a comfortable chair and you are looking at the center of the room and on the rug in front of you is a big dog. Let us call this dog a Boxer dog. This dog is different from most Boxer dogs because he is a Mexican Boxer dog. His nice brown

hair has black zebra stripes running over
his body - he is a Mexican Boxer dog.
The Mexican Boxer dog is lying there
curled up on the carpet in your living
room. You can see him very plainly.

Most Boxer dogs have a pushed in nose
and have trouble breathing. They snorkle
around and blow a bit, to get air. You
hear this gasping for breath and pulling
for air. This dog has been running in
the weeds and snow and the dirt; he is
wet. When dogs are wet they have a body
odor. O.K. Come back into the room.

What happened when you saw the dog on
the rug in your living room? Did you
each see him? You each saw the dog.
What did you see the dog with? Your eyes
were closed and you were sitting here in
this room. Your eyes were 20 miles or
more from your living room where the dog
was! How were you able to see the dog?
What are you seeing him with? Not your
eyes. What did you smell him with? Not
your nose! But some nose! That is right
... some nose. Did you hear him breath?

O.K. ... I am trying to show you that
your hearing, seeing, smelling senses are
right here in your physical body and yet
miles away you are able to see, to hear

20

and to smell. All of your five senses
are very active. They have to be the
senses on what we call the Astral body.
The Astral body is the body or sheath
Soul uses on the Astral plane; right here
on the spiritual world chart. All of
your sensory perception you will use in
the lower planes during an
out-of-the-body or Travel by Soul
experience will be done using the Astral
senses, not your physical senses. You
can sense everything that happens to you
this way. Sri Paul Twitchell describes
the astral senses as located about three
feet behind the head. You can see
hundreds of miles this way!

Now, the point I want to get to is that what you
saw was very real. You saw that dog lying there on
the carpet and it was very real to you. Since it was
very real to you, it must exist. And since it was
very real to you, it must exist someplace else. I
happen to know where that dog is and he does exist.
He is a beautiful Mexican Boxer dog. So, everything
that you do from now on is real and it does exist.
It does not matter whether we are doing things down
here on the earth plane or on one of the spiritual
planes or somewhere in the lower worlds. You have
just experienced it! You know it can be done, don't

you? You just did it!
   Now you have to develop that talent with
practice. Practice the ability to extend yourself
into other situations, other areas. Learn to control
your life. Learn to control your outer life into
your inner being.
   That is what we are trying to do, to be a DOER, to
make things happen. If we can control how we
function, we have it pretty well made. Our five
senses of sensory perception can exist wherever our
being is.
   Now, in order to become aware on the mind level,
we start off with certain things we carry along with
us. Our whole life is consciousness at this point
by: all the history we have read about in the past;
everything we have been taught in our society;
everything we have soaked up or smudged up; the
established groups or rules; ethics; mores; codes and
customs; hereditary things; are all kinds of hang-ups
we carry along as baggage.
   So right now we have to decide that we are going
to declare to ourselves that we are not going to be
afraid. We are not going to be afraid of the
unknown. Let us say that the unknown is all the
things which have been learned in our life which are
beyond our five senses' perception; the things where
we cannot see it, smell it, taste it type of things.
Everything beyond this sense is in the area of the
unknown. So now let us establish for ourselves that

we will not be afraid of any of these things.
Everything will be overcome somehow. Don't worry how
just now, just do it. You are not going to let
yourself be afraid of any of the things.
This also includes the fear of ridicule; fear of
the orthodox. Orthodox is the old standard or what
is acceptable; what society does; and this kind of
thing. We are told that we will be judged by our
peers because of the orthodox. You have to say to
yourself that you will separate yourself from
somebody else's control. You will not let them judge
you, or at least say that you will not accept their
judgement of you. You have to do this to free
yourself of the hang-ups we have been taught which
control us.

The next thing that is an obvious part of
awareness is the awareness of past karmic lives and
how they influence our present. In the Ancient
Spiritual Teaching we are aware of karma, however,
many teachings do not talk about it at all. When you
work on the relationship of Soul to mind you realize
that mind comes and goes with each life cycle;
whereas, the Soul is permanent and it goes on
forever. It never ceases or begins.

Karma is actually your actions and your
reactions. It is anything that is related to cause
and effect. We accept the karmic debt at the
beginning of each lifetime, and add onto it the karma
of the present lifetime. In the meantime you add

23

your day to day karma. Karma is the cause and effect
of your action and reaction. The karmic law is the
spiritual law which is dominate in the lower or
Second Grand Division of creation. The law of cause
and effect says "for everything that happens, there
is a cause." The effect is the result or the
reaction to it. As long as we are acted upon by some
outside force or cause, we are never really managing
our own affairs. Someone is influencing us and
affecting us to be and do things they want done. We
transgress, if we want to use that word, against
God's program every time we violate some of these
basic spiritual laws. When we view karma in the
context of Christianity and especially that of the
Catholics, when one dies as a Catholic, he is prayed
for by a priest to get that person out of purgatory.
Purgatory is a half-way house concept where the
person's sins must be removed to allow the person to
go on to heaven. Sin includes many things done both
against God and against other people and even against
the social order of accepted government. During the
reformation era of Christianity, the local priest or
constabulary established what sins were.

I don't recognize sin as such. I don't get into
this mental bind and hassle. If there is something
that has happened to me in this life or a previous
life, I can change it. I am the only one who can
change it and if I do not change it, nobody can.
Karma is a debt so called when you die under the

common belief and it must be dealt with. This is a pretty big load to stick on anybody. When we think of that sweet little baby who comes into this lifetime with a debt like that, he is already behind the 8-ball and there is no obvious way the baby can survive under that kind of load.

There are several reasons, when one works with the concept of sin, that make it unacceptable. Those sins that are earthly, are themselves created by the law of cause and effect and are the step-child of the creating Soul. There is no way for a priest or any third party to intervene. We can therefore accept that part we know of as karma and you and I can handle our problem and resolve it for ourselves. When we are ready to translate from this life into another form of existence, we hope that we have it neutralized, balanced or cancelled out.

Karma can effect you in a lot of ways and as long as you are reacting to things you are going to react to whatever your karmic pattern demands. Think of things you do almost automatically and do not change from week to week. You respond to things the way you know you should, not for any other reason. This is very detrimental because it prevents you from altering your life and changing your life to live a pure and good life as God and Soul would like you to do. You have to get your karma pushed aside somehow; not eliminated, just understand it and know how to deal with it.

The basic part of awareness is the sensory strength and impressions by our five senses. As soon as something happens to us in our awareness, the sensory strength is felt. If something is hurting, for example, how much is it hurting? Was it a pinch? Was it a burn hurt? What did you sense when you became aware of some condition or thing? When the mind reached out on the physical plane with the five senses, the mind is limited to the 36 symbols (dies) as inputs and if mind can't get it that way, it will not get it at all. The mind has to accept that situation or condition. The only other input that mind can get is an input from Soul. Awareness then depends on the strength of our impressions from the five senses.

Awareness is determined by the effect of the impressions that you sense. The sense of urgency is obtained this way, and danger reactions and protective response taken come to you by the effect awareness has.

You need awareness to provide an understanding of what was sensed and what happened. Like we mentioned earlier; if it was a pinch, or a burn, or puncture type of hurt; whatever kind of hurt it is, the awareness helps to understand it, as does the force of the impressions. This understanding comes across from the mental function to the Soul. It tells you (Soul) what caused it as a reality. The understanding of it gives you the reality of it.

This is where reality occurs, between the mind and Soul. On the higher levels we use other higher level senses and would have a higher level awareness of it. But, here we are concerned with physical awareness.

The interesting thing is that as soon as you understand what caused it, then you know! Oh boy! Now we have the knowing or the knowledge of it; we have the reality of what is happening; and we have gone full circle! We are right back to Soul again. Soul caused it and we have reality of it in Soul.

Awareness exists on the higher levels also. Let us briefly look at these. The five senses that we visualized the dog with as he lay on the carpet are the inner eyes, ears, nose, etc. You are sensing everything on the level where you exist at the moment. And you have to live within the state of awareness, wherever it is.

A good author can give you, or explain to you, all the sensory perceptions he needs to have you understand what he is saying. He is trying to have your senses convey the perceptions for you. The consciousness that the author has at the time he writes the words is that you are trying to perceive with your senses here and now.

When that author writes fiction, it is real to Soul as it exists as a perception of Soul. Writers use the term "fiction" to categorize a type of writing which is not based on fact. However, if you

are aware of all the things that go into your state
of consciousness wherever you are doing it, or
whatever you are doing, then it is real.

You have an understanding of it and it develops a
state of consciousness for you. This is the state
that gives you the private universe within. It is
that private area, the world you must learn to
control. When we have learned to control the inner
private universe within, we have mastered our life!
Every desire that we have can be realized. The
Holograms of Soul technique provides the means of
creating things by becoming CAUSE and those things
will become manifest by the sound current and the
pure laser light of the hologram; the object is
formed for you.

Being aware and having the reality is very
difficult to understand. When I speak to a group of
people and the chelas sit there in their chairs and
nod in agreement with what I am saying, I wonder if
you understand it yet? Has the message of awareness
really come across to you? I would like to do
something dramatic again. If I punched you in the
nose, you might get the reality of it, maybe?

I will punch each of you in the nose - SPLAT -
SPLAT. Now let us analyze what happened. I had an
idea that I was going to punch you. I got the idea
in mind, but the idea had to originate from Soul,
because all ideas and thoughts come from Soul. We
said that mind is not capable of doing that - it is

limited by the 36 symbols, right? Then what happened?

Something interesting happened to this thought when it entered the mind. Soul had to establish some neat things. It had to make an image of that thought or idea. Soul had to establish that it was going to punch you in the nose with my fist. We call this a thought form when we give it the form of a fist. Now this is a definite form and will manifest as a fist. Now, what else happened? This thought now has the form of a fist and the thought form comes down to the Astral plane. We know the Astral plane as the place where emotional feeling is given to the thought.

The thought picks up certain characteristics of how the thought will be felt. The feeling involved, is very important in the area of expression. The Astral will determine what kind of a hurt it will be. Is it going to hurt at all? Is the punch going to miss, or is it going to be right on the button? Here is a situation where you have a feeling of hurt, pain or anguish on impact. What else happened?

The thought is given the form of a fist. It is going to smash and bruise. It will have all those feelings involved. When mind comes over and delivers, you feel the blow, feel the force and you may have a bloody nose from it. There is a reality of the blow being delivered. This reality exists on the crossover on Chart 2 between mind and Soul.

A boxer will defend himself and when you are in

this kind of situation Soul will protect itself,
preserve itself. This is a survival thing by Soul.
Soul will not allow itself to be destroyed. There is
no way you can destroy Soul because Soul will take on
all kinds of forms, but it will not be destroyed.
Soul has to do this kind of thing; a good counter
puncher will bob and weave and will do all kinds of
moves to avoid that blow. When it did land, the
reality of it is there. Most people will feel the
blow. If you did not feel the blow, your Soul placed
a thought form into mind that the blow missed and
Soul was protected. Those of you who threw up your
hands in front of your face were reacting to the
hurt.

Now, this is where you want to be. You can change
your life, friends; you do not have to be punched in
the nose by everyone that walks up and down the
street swinging at you. How beautiful it is! You
can create any situation in your life that you want.
If you do not want to be harmed, you do not want to
be harmed by somebody else, you can change the
environment to something completely different. This
is the way it works. You each did it and you proved
it works!

CHAPTER 3

LEARN TO EXPERIENCE THE TRUTH

It makes me very happy to be privileged to tell you about Travel by Soul. I get a big bang out of sharing with you the things we are discussing and this flow of the ECK comes down to you through me as the Channel and I get a thrill from it. I will tell you what happened after the last discussion in Chapter 1 ... I didn't sleep at all that night. I was lying in bed, resting, but I did not sleep at all. That is the kind of high I get from it - it is exciting to me. It just lifts me up to an elevation that is inspiring!

Those things we discussed in Chapter 1 and 2 cover the most important background and tools you need to bridge across from your human position over into a spiritual area. It is very important because that is why we are here. Each of us is trying to pick ourselves up by the bootstraps and get ourselves going somewhere in a spiritual life. Therefore, we will review to make sure the importance has been emphasized.

One of the things I asked you to do was to take on a questioning attitude and I want you to learn to ask your questions to get your answer. Somebody may ask the same question but he will get a different answer that is right for him. That answer is given to him for the position he occupies in his spiritual

opening, wherever he happens to be at that time. In
the Shariyat I Sri Paul writes about asking
questions. This should be clarified to remove any
misunderstanding that may exist.

The thing we are asked not to do is that we must
not ask questions of DOUBT about the functions of the
Spirit. We ask questions of inquiry as we are trying
to learn. That is the type of question we should
ask. When you stop to think about it, why should you
question the Truth? How can you question the
authority of Supreme Deity? From that, we realize
that we should not be asking that kind of question.
It is not that we question what the Spirit is
performing, we have to accept that. You ask the
question that helps you to move along; that helps you
understand something about your spiritual experience;
you ask the kind of questions that motivate and
propel it along so that you have the rounded out and
complete understanding of it. I have had spiritual
people tell me, "Oh, no, you cannot ask questions,
that is a mental trip you are on." I have proven by
experience that the opposite is true.

Throughout Sri Paul's writing he tells us to ask
the question. Paul asks us to be curious. Jesus
said it when he was preaching about the same thing.
He said, "to come to me as little children." Jesus
did not mean that you had to be a five year old! He
meant that you had to come with the attitude of a
little child, that hunger for knowledge, that

curiousness, that longing type of inquiry. That is what we are trying to get. So, if we can make this distinction by staying on the right side of this issue and ask the correct questions we will be alright. You will get your hand slapped a few times by the Inner Master. I had mine bruised up pretty badly before I learned the difference; nobody told me of this. I am trying to pass it on to you so you can spare yourself some heartache!

We drew a chart that depicts all the God worlds up above the fifth plane and we called it the First Grand Division. Then we drew the Second Grand Division which is the mental and physical worlds. This is the creation which is referred to in the Bible, book of Genesis. In the Second Grand Division we show a "T" with Soul on one side and mind on the other side.

From the fifth plane down, we have the situation where the Soul and mind both exist. This is where we have all of our big problems, because we cannot separate them easily. We went into a discussion on how we tried to push mind aside and get mind out of the way. In Shariyat I we read that the greatest obstacle man must deal with is himself. If we can learn to handle our mind, get it pushed off to the side, and disciplined, then we have room for our Soul to shine through into our daily life.

We talked about how to discipline the mind. We mentioned several things. By trying to bring

33

together the lower self and the higher self, to make them one, in order to enter into the God worlds of Spirit, brings about defeat. They do not mix, and none are farther apart in poles than these two qualities. The lower self represents the KAL, which is the negative power. The higher self, Soul, represents the Spirit, which is the higher power. The twain shall never meet. On the lower, the universal mind power must step aside and be left behind with the physical body so that Soul can enter into the heavenly worlds. That is where we are. We have the duality between Soul and mind and we have to do something with that mind power.

Remember, we said we have to give mind something to work with; we had to give it some little task to keep it busy and then let Soul do its thing. We wanted to find some way to put Soul in charge of our mind and we explored several ways we could do that.

We next reviewed the spiritual exercise as we know it in the Ancient Spiritual Teaching. When you are on the path of the Ancient Spiritual Teaching, you are told you have to look within your inner being to find the Spiritual Master. He will lead you and teach you. You can do this as you have been told, by looking into the third eye which is located in the forehead between the physical eyes. Close your eyes and focus your attention on that spot to a kind of small movie screen there. Your mind will flash all of its thoughts and everything that is coming before

34

it on that screen. You just have to push these
things off the screen to clear it. Say, I'm not
interested in that, I don't want to see that, or
don't want to talk about it, until the mind goes
blank.

I have found that if I sat there like a knot on a
stump, nothing ever took place, until I asked a
question. That is why I keep coming back to the
questioning technique. I ask for the Inner Master
Consciousness and the living Spiritual Master. Soon a
blue light appears. The Master comes in the form of
a blue light and this light covers everything around
me. This is pretty exciting when it happens. I
don't know what your reaction is going to be to this
but you will have a different one than I did because
you are an individual. Try this on for size and make
it work.

The point to nail down is one that most Spiritual
Students miss when they join the path of the Ancient
Teaching and they never seem to realize what is
happening. When you go into your inner eyes,
supposedly the screen that you are looking at is
right on your forehead. You can not possibly see it
with these physical eyes. The eyes cannot go back in
your skull and see it on the screen of the third
eye! So, you are looking at it with the Astral eyes,
which are located outside your skull about three feet
back of the head, Sri Paul Twitchell said.

You have to accept right then that you are doing

something pretty marvelous! You have gone outside of your body; you are looking with eyes beyond the body. You are looking through the body and this impresses the awareness of the mind. That is an important achievement. If you have not experienced something like that before, it's got to be a milestone for you!

We said the beginning awareness and the spiritual exercise you needed when you first joined the Ancient Spiritual Teaching, have changed. Your spiritual exercises have built you up to a certain point of awareness due to experience.

Your need then is different from your need now, today. Your need is to change and modify the exercise a bit to keep pace with you as you open up and grow and mature. You will need to do different exercises from what you did as a new initiate. For example, I hardly ever need to go into the inner eye to get an awareness. That was what I did fifteen years or so back. I think I have gone beyond that in my evolvement. When you start out, you do need it. So, be aware of change and allow yourself to change. Move along with what is working for you. If going through the third eye works for you, and it will work the first few times you start it, for goodness sake keep it up. Don't cast it away, but make it function and continue to perform for you until you need something else. You can then do other things.

We discussed the ability to contemplate.

Contemplation is different from meditation.
Meditation is what the yogi does. The yogi places
himself in a relaxed position hoping that some great
truism will come to him. Well, if you have an active
twentieth century mind, you mind is not going to sit
idle. It is not going to remain blank for long.
Little children have a concentration span of only a
few seconds before they are distracted. As we grow
older, we can keep our minds blank for maybe five
minutes. If you are in a position standing in the
corner or doing some lotus position or something like
that, sooner or later the mind is going to crowd in
and have all the mental trash recirculating. The
spiritual benefit will be washed away. This
meditation is very passive.

Let us do what we call contemplation.
Contemplation is an activity where you are an active
participant by your control of it and you experience
the whole thing. Experience means that you have done
it and it is your own personal knowledge. This is
the thing that makes contemplation so important. We
need to ask those questions to make it happen. So,
we come back to the questions to be asked in the
child-like innocence, the desire to learn, the desire
to find out. You ask the questions you think you
should ask to know and it will start POPPING for
you. As long as you ask the questions you will get
the answers.

I am telling you that you are dealing in an area

of infinite and unlimited knowledge. GOD is
ALL-KNOWING, OMNISCIENT. When you ask a question,
BOOM, that answer is right there. Instantaneously it
is available to you. In fact, you cannot ask a
question if the answer is not already provided for
you. This seems funny, doesn't it? But that is a
fact! In order for you to ask the question, the
information has to be there already. You couldn't
question it if it weren't.

So, this is the kind of thing that you should
practice as none of us are expert at it. It is not
going to happen overnight. We have to learn to do
it. You have spent thousands and millions of
lifetimes in the past and you have stumbled over this
thing and have fallen on your face. You have not
done it yet. You have not gotten back to the God
world! So, we have each made a lot of mistakes and
now we have another opportunity to do it. This is
the kind of thing that will start making it work.
Contemplation is the way you can have a spiritual
experience. You won't have a spiritual experience
doing the yogi bit. It just won't work because the
yogi acts entirely within the universe of mind.
Contemplation acts within the spiritual areas with
Soul. Contemplation is a veritable bonanza. Here is
something that you can really get your teeth into and
start working with and thinking about.

Let me share an experience with you which I had
that will illustrate the whole thing. It ties in

with the use of Astral senses, asking questions and it gives a nice rounded out feeling of it.

Many years ago, about 15-20 years ago, it was Christmas time. We were having the great big Christmas scene.T.V., churches and everything and everyone was laying the Christmas trip on us, the thing we get each year. All the hymns, songs, the radio announcers and everyone talking about the Christmas message. There is always the manger scene with the baby Jesus and mother Mary, and off in the shadows somewhere is a poor guy that never gets any credit for anything, called Joseph.

Soon, three men come in off camels with all kinds of riches and incense and they are called Wise Men. Well, this bothered me this particular year. I was filled up to my eyes with this kind of thing. I started to ask myself questions like, Wise Men? Who said they were wise? Where are the Wise Men? Are the Wise Men all around? I don't see any today. When I go to the inner contemplation I don't see any Wise Men. Who are these people? What makes them so wise? Well, I was

39

asking this kind of question and asking
to have my questions answered. All of a
sudden I was up in the sky over the city
of Jerusalem. It was dark at night and as
I circled around Jerusalem, looking down
at it a big shaft of light came from high
up above somewhere. It illuminated what
was going on down there in Jerusalem.

Now the light illuminated the city and
I could see. There was one fellow
mending some tools, and tarps. There was
another man preparing some food over a
fire, but no Wise Men. So, I asked my
guide when I first saw this scene, "What
am I looking at?" (This is the kind of
question to ask.) I found out what this
group was and who they were and why they
were there. The next question I asked my
guide was, "Where do they get their
information or their knowledge, from the
Wise Men"? Where does this light come
from - this light which lights up the
campground? I was moved instantaneously
right over into the shaft of light. My
friends, this was a tremendous
experience!

The shaft of light came down through
the back of my head. Then it split or
divided into two shafts of light at my

two eyeballs. Two columns of light went
down to the herdsmen in Jerusalem. I was
still trying to find out who the Wise Men
were. I was instantaneously given the
whole wash of knowing-knowledge. That
light coming from above, from the
heavenly worlds, was going through me!
The light of their world was coming
through me!!
I could see in the center of my skull,
which was filled with light. I was
viewing this with my Astral senses. The
blood vessels on the inside of my skull
were all there and my two eyeballs were
both there and I could see the light
shining right through my eyes with my
Astral senses. The knowing and knowledge
which I received is my private little
universe within. I will not reveal that
to you - but what happened and what
brought it about is appropriate here.

This experience happened to me when I was living
in California and I was sharing it with a fifth
initiate of the Ancient Spiritual Teaching in Seattle
several years later, and she said, "Well, Bert, don't
you think that is a bit prophetic"? I replied that I
didn't know. The point is that my questions were
answered in such a dramatic way that the whole

rounded out understanding of the question was given to me. To learn to use the inner senses we will have to work on it repeatedly.

That is the kind of result one can get from contemplation when one asks the first question, the next question, and the next question. When we discussed the instantaneous flash of insight, this is the method you can use to enlarge and extend the insight to make the insight grow into a full experience! The flash insight will take on new aspects for you.

We were going to set some goals or objectives for ourselves. I hope you have actually sat down and tried to think about your goals? What are you trying to do? Where are you trying to go with yourself? How do you expect to get there? What do you expect to see when you get there? The mind needs this kind of discipline so that it has some good constructive things to remember.

Knowing the mind and the mental functions is very important and a small review is indicated. The twenty-six letters and the ten numerals are the total capability of the mind. That is the total limitation of the mind also. Mind can do nothing without these 36 symbols. Mind has no ability to think: no ability to generate new thoughts. The ideas all come from Soul to the mind.

If you can just get this concept of limitation into your thinking and keep it, then we can start to open up avenues of doing more things, bigger things, than you ever thought possible. These 36 symbols limit what the mind does and if you allow them to control you, that is as far as your limitation will take you. There is no way that you can ever see, or understand, or perceive, or do anything with God, with a stupid mind that can only work with these 36 symbols! You cannot explain God in your language at all!

What we are talking about here are all the spiritual types of things, the esoteric things, on all the levels where Soul dwells. There is no vocabulary to describe this! Now if mind needs something to do and something to guide it, we have to provide some input from Soul, some ideas from Soul to replace the mind recorded memory.

Remember, I suggested to you that you stop or change your goal from seeking God? Seeking God is the thing we have all been doing all of our lives. Some of us persist and still seek God after we are initiated to the second, third or fifth circle. Seeking is the act of beseeching God for something; you make demands on God; or try to exploit God. In other words you Pray to God. Prayer will not do it. There is no way prayer will accomplish what you need to accomplish.

I am asking you to change from seeking God to a position of serving God. This is a whole new attitude for us. To serve God you become the master of your

43

every-day life. Through the Ancient Spiritual
Teaching you can do just that. The Ancient Spiritual
Teaching gives you the tools; it points the way; it
gives you the means to change your life. Master
those things in your daily life, keep evolving,
growing, getting higher and higher on the spiritual
planes in spiritual activity. And that is what the
whole experience of Travel by Soul is all about,
lifting yourself up into these other areas. There
are many activities in your life you have to master
as you go along. It will not happen BOOM, BOOM. You
have to develop with it.

So, again I would like to recap that by saying, to
master your life, you must be a DOER of God's words.
You have to do God's work - not the work of the
mind. As soon as you cease to be a DOER and are not
doing what the Spirit is telling you to do or should
be done, what happens? You revert back to being a
searcher, again. We may be just a believer. If we
just believe something, that is completely passive.
Religions all tell us to "believe". Man, you've got
to believe! They give you nothing else.

We discussed those things with which the mind
functions. The five senses like seeing, smelling,
hearing, touching, and tasting and the ideas from
Soul. As long as we are content to live within the
mind realm we are doomed to sit in our misery and
suffering. Sometimes we get a glimmer of light
across our awareness and that is reality. The thing

44

that happens is the idea from Soul caused something to happen in the mind. The idea effected you in such a way that you became aware of the idea in your mind. It is very important to get this awareness of what is happening in the mind.

One of the primary spiritual laws of this lower life that we are living in, is the law of cause and effect. This law states that for everything that is done or achieved or accomplished, there is something that caused it. The cause came from Soul. Soul caused something to happen and you experienced the happening in your outer life or environment sensed by your five physical senses. When the cause came across, you perceived the little insight that came from Soul, that is where you want it to be. We want to be able to perceive what is real that occurs in Soul.

So, it might be helpful to review that discussion we had on the Mexican Boxer Dog. It is very important that you realize that you sensed the dog with your spiritual senses and not your physical senses and that this awareness opens up all the spiritual worlds to you - everything that exists in the spiritual world is now available to you! NOW! You know where the spiritual senses are and you can start to use them on the inner planes. See everything where ever it happens to be on the higher levels. Start to work on that concept. Be aware of what is happening to you when this happens.

45

Awareness is the ability to retain what we experienced on the level where our BEING exists. When you go into the higher levels in your out-of-body experience, you will have a retention of where you have been, what you have done, what importance it was, what it meant and all about it.

We talked about the reality of things that were happening on this level and the way the awareness came to us in the mind. If you have forgotten this or if some time has elapsed since you read the dramatic demonstration of being punched in the nose, go back and reread it. Some people were hurt by the blow and reality of it came to the mind and the awareness of it was obvious. We are working on the mental plane where the mind is dominant. This is the area of physical reaction, the law of cause and effect.

Soul determined what effect the blow would have. Soul is eternal and cannot be destroyed. Soul will not allow itself to be destroyed. So instead of letting people hurt you, let Soul take care of it, put it into the Spirit for solution. Soul will take whatever deviate means are necessary to protect itself and preserve itself to survive.

You are learning to provide spiritual control of your mind and to put those ideas into the mind that you want to be there. Life can be beautiful, serene, harmonious, and have all the color and vivid beauty that you want it to have. You don't have to go on

living in all the dirt and muck and filth and rape
and sadistic stuff that comes from earth. That is
the name of the game, to learn to control mind!

Now we will talk about TRUTH.

Truth is a big thing. Truth has to be a real heavy
weight! Any discussion of Truth must be approached
from Travel by Soul because any other angle just gets
confusing. Truth has been a hard concept to grasp,
hard to understand, it has been very evasive. Truth
is one tremendous thing. "What greater gift could be
given to you than to be told the Truth that would set
you free"? I think this statement is in the
Christian Bible - but the Bible never does anything
with Truth. The Bible does not have the means to
bring it about. This is up to you to bring Truth
into your life and make it happen.
    I have never seen the subject of Truth treated in
any of the religions. The Ancient Spiritual Teaching
provides this to us and it does it in this way. The
Truth that sets you and me free in Spirit is that you
and I can experience in imagination what we desire to
experience in reality. Let me explain that. The
Truth that sets you free, you will remember, is that
the Spirit is the word of God. So Truth is in the
Spirit and it is all wrapped up in it. The Truth
that sets you free in Spirit is that you can

47

experience in your imagination what you desire to experience in reality. When you maintain this experience in imagination, your desire becomes a reality. This is what we have been trying to do. We are trying to experience Truth and have it on this reality plane, here on the Chart 2 between Soul and mind. By doing it in imagination we image it or give our thought form!

We need to talk about imagination next.

Imagination is the only way to pursue and find Truth. You will never find Truth unless you approach it through imagination! I met a Madis (a fifth initiate of the Ancient Spiritual Teaching) who told me that he didn't think there was much to this Travel by Soul thing, that he thought it was just the normal opening or evolution of Soul. I just don't understand this kind of reasoning. Paul says that you cannot arrive by any other means! You have to arrive at the Truth through imagination. It is the only way. When I read Paul's statement, I want to learn all I can about imagination and I pay attention to it. This kind of misunderstanding must be clarified. This is an example of the grand Cop-Out of the Ancient Spiritual Teaching!

This is right where we have to be. We have to learn about imagination. The basic or root word of imagination is image or i-m-a-g-e. Now this brings us right back to thought forms. The thought form comes from Soul shown on Chart 2 and we have to learn

now to image things. The image is the whole wrapped
up in the gamut of cause and effect. It is the
spiritual law of cause and effect. If we can
understand that one principle, we have come a long
way. The Cause and the Effect **is** the Thought and the
Thing.
Let us go further into our discussion of
imagination. There are several points that are quite
important about imagination. One important thing is
the aspect of feeling. If we have certain feelings,
it would change the whole image, or the whole thought
form. When we don't like the feeling that we are
getting, if we are getting pain and hurt and we don't
want to be pained or hurt, we can image another idea,
another thought form that "doesn't let the blow
land." Then it doesn't hurt at all. See how
wonderful this is? It works! You just did it, each
of you did it! You know it works!
As you did it, you expressed enthusiasm. I guess
you have noticed how enthusiastic I get when we are
talking about it. There is an aspect of feeling
known as enthusiasm and we can get all fired up over
this aspect. I have never found anything like this
before anywhere, and enthusiasm is a great part of
the feeling.
Another part of feeling is attitude. Attitude
comes in to play when we determine how we are going
to present our questions. We mentioned that we had
to come with an attitude of a little child; the

loving, innocent, trusting, inquiring, curiosity of a small child. If you have that kind of attitude, you can receive the wonderful things of Soul. Instantaneously. You will have this wonderful knowing inside!

A certain attitude can put you in touch with the Knowing power. When you establish the attitude of a curious child-like devotion to the Supreme Deity, and when you hold this devotion for a period of time, contact with Truth will manifest. It will appear on the physical earth for you, or on the spiritual plane, wherever your Being exists. You can become the operator of the power by Soul's direction. This is just where I am trying to lead you, to the point where you can operate with the Spirit power. You can make things happen for yourself and create anything you want. All those things in your outer world can be created in this manner. Things like houses, cars, everything you want to create is provided to you. You can now establish imagination as a basis for your life.

The association of ideas is a habit factor in imagination. Let us think of how the habit is formed from association. When you have an idea coming across your mind from Soul, here on the Chart 2, what happens? Can you think of things with boundaries? The boundaries of a page of paper or this book, for example, are 5 1/2 X 8 1/2 inches. The boundaries of this room, we are all inside this room and it has

50

dimensional boundaries. These are examples of ideas that have association limitations on them. We can also think of certain categories or groups. We associate people to races, countries, and many kinds of related groups. Think of birds such as the quail. You have to think of quail as a whole covey of quail. You hardly ever see just one quail at a time. The quail are associated together.

We believe what might be determined for us by our outer senses. Now, our outer senses working in the mind area develops a whole bunch of stuff for us and we are inclined to accept that. We do not seem to question it. We allow this bunch of thoughts to permeate our life. It just goes into many things we do. Habit guides us to picturize the life of ourself.

When we picture the life style of a farmer, for example, that is what you picture or image for yourself. The thoughts come over as those things that a farmer is and does and this materializes in the physical world in the mind and all five senses support it as being real. You are a farmer. You are an orchardist with an orchard. You are a civic leader of something. You even have the ability to fail and you can picture yourself as a failure. This is a group consciousness of your outer senses that forms your life pattern and you accept it. You picturize (image) it and you live it. It may or may not be good.

These things become a part of your inner being or
your private universe. No one else has any way of
knowing what it is. People who are composers and
write beautiful music compose from their inner
universe. People write poetry from their inner
universe, for example, Blake or Yeats, or Ralph Waldo
Emerson, who in his essays on the theme that the
world as we know it as being plastic, with no form or
substance. The thing that gives it substance is
you. You put your attention on it and bring the
Light and Sound energy on it down through you and
form manifests for you on the physical plane in your
environment. Not my environment, yours. Each of us
create our own environment this way. We bring the
object into the Present moment or the NOW OF TIME.
   If you are a sane person or what is normally
called a sane person, you must be able to control
those things in the mind area. If you are insane,
you are blown away by the material thing and you are
controlled by events and circumstances that other
people have created; or that other governments have
created; or that an entity or someone else has
created and you are subject to them. You are
controlled by it. You have lost! You are what many
people classify as insane. This should have a lot of
meaning. It is very vivid. You have to learn to
control all of this stuff. You have to control
matter; all the things in your physical world is
matter. You see matter as an extension of your

imagination, friends, it is right here on our Chart 2
between Soul and mind. When you see matter as an
extension of your imagination then you can master
life. You can control life and everything starts.
Then the events become sunshine and roses for you.
We are trying to show that all this control comes by
providing the ideas from Soul. The pure beautiful
ideas from Soul. The <u>God</u> <u>word</u> <u>ideas</u> from Soul and
making them manifest for us!

On the Spiritual Worlds Chart 1 as we go up on
those other planes, wherever you happen to be going
on the Travel by Soul trip, that is where you are at
that instant. You are experiencing that thing at
that level. We have discussed the importance of
setting goals. Goals are necessary to establish the
direction your energy is going. If you have not set
a goal, your energy is going to be dispersed. It is
going to be weak since it is not concentrated on
anything specific and it won't give you much.

You should generate a goal and change the goal
within a certain period of time so that once you
achieve a certain awareness you can go on to
something else. Keep setting goals for yourself. As
often as you get close to completion of a goal,
overlap with another goal so you are always
directed. Your energy will not be scattered or
diffused. When you want to go on a Travel by Soul
trip, make a plan; set goals; and know where you
expect to be and what you want to accomplish.

We will now consider memory of past lives, and past failures.

Failure seems to impress us more than success. You can readily forget the nice things that happen, but you remember the horrible and the bad things. They stay with you all of your life. Things that happen to you as a child you remember but the nice things like the beautiful sunny days are forgotten. The KAL makes sure the negative things keep returning in our outer being as long as it can.

We have unconscious types of devices that create laziness and a lack of incentive, etc. When you have the goal there and energy goes to achieve the goal and this other stuff gets very little attention.

Now we will talk about TRUTH.

We have been talking about what makes up Truth. Truth is imagination. Truth is happening right here on this plane as well as all the planes above. To start off, Truth has been the most sought after and the most evasive thing in history. Down through all of history there is a record of people searching for Truth. They have been looking for the "Fountain of youth", searching for Truth. They have been looking for "Somebody that has the Light." They have been looking for the "Swami from the East" to tell them the Truth. With all this banging around , the Truth has avoided them. We have found out now how we can make Truth happen through imagination, imaging, and forming images. So, you have the tools to find Truth and to make it BE for you.

I want to tell you what I know about Truth. Truth is Knowing. I am not concerned here with what Truth applies to, the Truth is Knowing. When we have the feeling of knowing, OH BOY! OH MAN! You have arrived!! Nothing can kick you around. Nothing can distract you because - You Know! That is why I do not hesitate to come before you and write about the Truth, because no one can come up and argue with me or challenge me on what I am telling you because I know it is the Truth. I don't have to question it. I know.

Spiritual Reality is the Truth and understanding is evasive and difficult because we cannot get a mental picture of it. This is the problem of the mind due to its limitation of the 36 symbols of language. Language exists only on the level of mind through which mind tries to express itself vocally to the external world. Truth is beyond the mental realm and it cannot be grasped through external vision. When you saw the Mexican Boxer Dog, you saw it through the internal vision. You were seeing it truthfully. You were experiencing Truth. You come to the point where you must accept that the Truth IS, and nothing more. You must find your own way to God. No one can do this for you. I cannot do it for you. Nobody else can. You have to get a hold and start forming the images from Spirit so that you can Know.

In the relationship of Soul to God, Soul can never

achieve equivalence with God the Supreme Deity. Soul must be content to grasp only a particle of the totality of the Supreme Deity. Soul can realize IT more completely by knowing and experiencing the God-state and by linking up the Truth in such a way that the knower and the known are one. This is a fine line of understanding, when your existence is on a higher plane, the awareness of the happening and the observer is the same thing. These two things (Soul and the happening) are of God, the same. This concept may be more fully explained for you in a later section in this book dealing with Holograms of Soul.

Every time that I have been on a Travel by Soul experience, no matter what level I was on, the message always came to me as a Knowing. When I saw the Jewish herdsman taking care of their sheep near Jerusalem, this knowing came through. It did not come through as a language. It did not come through as symbols. It came through as a Knowing. It floods over you. It takes you in. You know there is something there and you have the complete understanding of it. If there is still something you do not understand, ask another question and get the rest of the knowing picture. As long as you can ask questions, you will get the knowing, and Boy OH Boy, I think that is great!

Use of the techniques of Traveling by Soul should prove to each of us that Truth is a different Reality for each person. Truth is a variation of experiences and we cannot set a standard for it. There are no words to describe Truth since Truth is in the esoteric realm. We are down here on the mind level on our Chart 2. I cannot tell you what Truth is because I cannot express it or convey it in the 36 symbol language. I can tell you that it is a beautiful Knowing. You have to experience it for yourself.

As your Travel by Soul continues to emphasize and strengthen Soul, the importance and strength of mind is diminished until mind must learn that it is temporary and cannot exist since it belongs to the Kal Niranjan. Soul, on the other hand, does not belong in the lower worlds, except as a temporary co-habitant with mind (Chart 2) and its communication is with the Spirit, the word, the Sound. Your biggest problem is yourself, your mind. You have to get mind under control, get mind out of your way. You can look at this another way. Since there is no greater problem, once you have mind out of the way and under control, it is an open road for you to travel from there on, and you have the whole God Reality ahead of you.

Each of us is tested according to our capacity and we are not tested beyond it. I think that is great. You don't have to worry about being stuck out on a limb and never get back. You don't have to worry about the things the yogis and the psychologists, and

57

all the junk the medical profession throws at you in the psychological field, because that stuff does not exist. It will never happen to you.

When I was in school as a child I was afraid that I would be examined in one of my courses in school and I would be asked a question I could not answer. This would be embarrassing. Then, I realized there wasn't a teacher or a professor or anybody that is going to ask me a question I cannot answer. I am never going to be tested beyond my capability, or my capacity. When you are Traveling by Soul, you don't have to worry about being exposed to things you cannot handle. You will never be asked to do it.

When we were considering starting up a series of discussion sessions, and we were talking about how we were going to do it, who would be invited to attend, etc. My position was - Hey, I am not in that kind of business. I am not going to determine who is to come and who is not going to come. The Living Spiritual Master and the Supreme Deity has determined that each of you should be there. Those people who aren't there, I cannot be too concerned about. They are not ready. They are not capable of understanding it or cannot handle it now. They are not there and that is where it stands.

We arrange to get ourselves to places we have to be and we are never exposed to things we cannot handle. Doesn't that make you feel kind of warm inside? It makes me feel like I am beginning to get a hold of myself and I don't have to be afraid of anything. I don't have any peers who are going to make judgements of me, they cannot control me. If they try I will come in with some nice attitude of ideas, like "I enjoyed hearing you talk about me, thank you." I don't have to defend myself or argue with them. That is already taken care of.

The question has been asked if I would clarify the association of ideas with imagination. Imagination is made up of several aspects. Association of ideas is one of those aspects or groupings with which the mind works. Where imaginative ability or the ability to create an image is involved, there are several things that allow you to form an image. I have given you this idea of the thought form as a way to image and that is the easiest way to understand it. We can take the idea and give it a form. Our mental process will do this automatically when the idea is entered into mind and if the mind does not have an instant form for the idea, mind will use an association of things or groupings of ideas to form it. It will make the image look similar to something it has in memory storage. One idea suggests another, etc. If we play that parlor game of naming all those things you know of colored yellow, for example, without any definite object or image, the mind will flash all kinds of images until something stops it on one of them.

The question has been asked when we are Astral

traveling, and you go some place, can somebody else
actually see your body there? No, you don't take
your body along. They see your spirit body or they
perceive the presence of your spirit. I will give
you an example of this.

I have a friend whom I introduced to
the Ancient Spiritual Teaching a few
years ago. He went back east to live and
he met a lady and fell in love and they
decided to get married. They phoned me
from Michigan State to ask me to attend
their wedding. I said I would be there
in my spiritual body. His wife-to-be has
been in the Ancient Spiritual Teaching
several years and she exclaimed to him,
"Why, there is Bert. He got to our
wedding alright." We have never met, and
she did not know what I looked like
physically. I have not seen her
physically and do not know what she looks
like, but she saw me and knew it was me.
She was aware of my presence.

CHAPTER 4

LEARN WHAT CONSCIOUSNESS IS

We have been developing some tools to learn how to
do things. Let us see how you are applying them. If
you want something to happen, you have to get in and
make it work. I know that each of us has a problem
to apply these tools to a good advantage. I do too,
I have to work on it continually. Sometimes the
answers come to me in strange ways. It seems to be
appropriate to discuss some of the things that we've
been talking about to see if we can really use them.
    I have mentioned this thing of picturing and
imaging and I know this is a difficult thing to do.
It really is difficult to learn how to picture things
because nothing in your education, your schooling or
social life teaches you how to image. You have to
learn this, you have to want it, and you have to try
it. Some mathematicians and some scientists
unknowingly do teach the principle but don't know its
meaning. Descriptive geometry teaches the student to
see the object, to rotate if mentally 30 degrees
horizontally, and rotate it 90 degrees in the
vertical axis, and then draw the picture of it.
    Whenever you think of a thought, you should not
just think the thought as a mental exercise, but
image it. Just be conscious of this and try to image

it. What is it you really want to see, what is it
you really want to do and form the image of it.

This imagination characteristic or trait of
imagining things is a behavior that is put down from
childhood. When a child seems to be getting far out
in his behavior and stares off out the window, for
example, he is accused of daydreaming and the parent
or teacher says, "don't do that." He is asked to
stop fantasizing and stop looking out the window.

Our schooling system is 180 degrees out of phase
with the way it should be. Schools should be going
in the opposite direction. We should be encouraging
our people to image. You have been put down and
taught not to image all your life. Now let us stop
catering to the negative aspects of the KAL and the
negative education that we have been getting, all the
negative junk that we have been fed all of our
lives. We have to turn around and recognize the
Supreme Deity is going to help us to get on the
positive approach and we have to learn those things
we have been taught not to learn. So when you learn
to put your thoughts in an image form, then you
create it. That is when the thrill starts coming for
you. Things all start happening the way you imaged
it!

What happens when you lose something? For
example, you lose your car keys? Why can't you find
them? So each of us has his own problem. You have
to analyze yourself to gain the self-consciousness of

what you did to make it disappear. There are two
sides to this imaging coin. There is the flip side
that says that when you don't image, then it doesn't
appear for you. If you do not image what you want to
have, what you want to materialize or manifest in
your physical life in the form of keys, it won't
happen for you. You won't see them; you won't find
them where you expect to find them. They won't be
there.

I was at the beach one time looking
for oysters. I had been to this beach
before and had found oysters lying around
on rocks as big as the palm of my hand.
I had just walked around with a gunny
sack and picked them up. I had a ball.
The next time I went to that beach, the
waves and the tide had come and gone, and
there were no oysters lying around on top
of the rocks. I thought something
strange had happened. I hunted around
for oysters, running around the beach
with my bag trying to find oysters. I
found one or two, but nothing
worthwhile. So, I finally stopped racing
around, and I figured out what had
happened.
Soon I realized I was looking for the

wrong thing. I had imaged oysters lying out on top of the ground and I did not find them there. So, I had to ask, "what would an oyster look like if it were standing up on edge between two rocks? Or in the sand"? Ah ... the little scalloped edge or ribbon line of the shell would be the only part exposed for me to see. When I looked for the little ribbon sticking up on edge in the sand, I began to see all kinds of oysters for they were just a few inches under the sand and sticking their little edge up out of the sand.

This is what you have to do. You have to ask what it is you want to see, what it is you are really looking for? How will you find this thing?

One day my son was gardening, and he had lost a large ring of keys in an area where he had raked out beauty bark over the flower beds. He was hopelessly lost and asked me to help find them. I pointed out to him that he could not expect to see the key ring lying out on top of the beauty bark, that he had looked over the ground and had not found

them there. Look for the edge of the
keys, sticking out of the bark, look for
a shiny spot reflecting from the sun,
maybe a piece of metal, look for things
like that. You know - BOOM, BOOM just a
matter of a few seconds and we had found
the keys. That is the kind of thing you
have to do.

You have to be innovative, you have to be
imaginative. Remember the first part of the word
imagination is image. When success happens to you
you get a lot of fun from it, you get all elated and
you can say, I did something right! Now what did you
do that was right? Go back and analyze yourself and
find out what you did to make it happen. It is
there, you caused it. Again, you have to understand
yourself and establish your self-consciousness with
what happened. This is what we were talking about
previously when our Soul crossed over into the mind
areas on our Chart 2 and caused it. What was it you
did to create it?

We have mentioned before that we are never
expected to do things beyond our capability, so don't
worry about what the considerations are. Just jump
into it and get doing it. The Supreme Deity never
subject you to things you can't handle or things with
which you can't cope. When you start to look for
possibilities to create things, just do it, and if

for some reason you are not able to do it or handle it, you will not be allowed to do it. When this happens, you will know. You will have the awareness and the knowledge that you were prevented from doing the action because, because, because, in other words, you are given the beautiful wash of knowing. Then you can correct yourself and get your act together the right way. Then when you do it again you won't have any trouble or problem.

The reason I mention this is if you have the ability to create things, you also have the ability to destroy and you should be aware of the dangers of destroying part of what has been created. When you lost something like the keys, and they do not manifest for you, what did you do? You destroyed it, didn't you? You did not allow it to come into your consciousness. You do this every day of your life and you did not know what was happening. If you do not want to destroy things, stop, analyze what you are doing and correct it. Put something else there and make your life beautiful. This is the kind of discipline that you start forming for yourself.

If somebody is bugging you, and you don't want to be bugged, or you can't get along with a person, get them out of your consciousness. Use your proper imaging. Caution should be taken not to harm the other person and do nothing that will cause you negative karma. As long as you realize that everything, and that means everything, that appears

in your outer world (in your environment) you
created, and only you are the the cause of it all.
Thereby you also have the power to remove and change
the environment as you wish!

But in effect, it is anti-creative; it is
non-creative. It is removing a creation from your
consciousness. So when you understand what you are
doing when destruction happens to you, you will not
be frightened by it. When you make an error and you
did not want to destroy it, you can bring it back
again - you can recreate it. When you do not wish to
destroy or remove an object from your environment,
merely image the more favorable thing or neutralize
the bad image with a positive acceptable thought
form. This is beautiful and it is possible because
you accept the full responsibility for your actions.

To leave the concept of destruction or destroying
things of creation open is not proper. We mentioned
it here so that you can develop a fuller
understanding of the created consciousness within
you. However, you must be aware that God, Soul, the
Spirit, the Word being perfect and eternal cannot
co-exist with things non-perfect or which can be
terminated or destroyed. You are permitted to use
creation (the states of consciousness) as long as
you do so for the betterment of all. When you start
to use the destructive power for self gain or
aggrandizement, as a tool of the Ego, you are
allowing yourself to fall back into the negative

worlds and you lose this ability and power. When any of the five passions come into action, your ability to perform constructive Travel by Soul is removed by the Inner Master! This can be proven to yourself by flipping a coin for heads. As long as you try to learn or understand the basic principle of it, it works. As soon as you try to profit personally by gambling, it stops.

A little more on the subject of Truth ...

In a review of Sri Paul's writings to see where he had really described Truth in any detail, I find that he says in one place that this is impossible to do. This is so because Truth is spiritual or esoteric and there is no language for it. The human language cannot describe Truth with the 36 symbols of our language which is completely physical and of the mind world.

I cannot describe Truth either, but as I mentioned before, the Truth that has come to me, has come in the form of KNOWING. Now it may come to you in a different way, I don't know, I cannot express that for you; but when I have a Travel by Soul experience, Truth comes through to me as a knowing. Wherever I find myself, I know all about it. The way that I have been able to attain that attitude is through the questioning approach. As long as I can ask questions, I get this wonderful wash of information.

Asking those questions is another technique we have to think about and learn to do because we get

our hands slapped each day for poking into areas
other people think we should not be and they say
things like, "Oh, get lost or something." Some times
they even swear at you. I have been sworn at many
times. I ask a lot of questions about things people
think I don't have the right to know or to ask. When
you ask your question, you get the answer you need
wherever you are, whatever your situation is. This
wonderful all knowledgeable, all knowing Supreme
Deity gives you what you need. I don't have any way
of knowing what you need to know. I don't even know
what I need to know. The Supreme Deity takes care of
each of us individually. And that is exciting when
you think about it. You are getting all this
individual insight and you must be somebody very
special. If you know when you know, you know it is
the Truth; and when you are sure about it when you
know, then you know you cannot dilute the Truth.
There are no more questions to ask about it. IT IS.
    Each person must experience Truth to understand
it. This is why the Ancient Spiritual Teaching is so
beautiful. Nothing else that I know of gives the
way, the path, to experience Truth. If I can
experience something, then it is mine. It isn't
anybody else's and I have it, it is part of me. The
knowing that you get of what "IS", is very
important. In your quest for this knowing your
questions may not be quite adequate. Your questions
might not be inclusive enough or they might not be

specific enough to get the answer you need. So you have to kind of poke around a bit. Keep yourself free and loose and ask good questions.

You can control your dreams this way. When you start dreaming, ask your questions and take control of the dream. You can get the purpose of the dream, the reasons for the dream, and the whole experience of the dream is provided for you to get the meaning for you. When we talk about Travel by Soul, to whom do we ask these questions? You always have a guide with you, you are never alone. Your guide is the Inner Master and he is always with you. Ask him all those questions and he is right at your elbow or your shoulder. The Master will tell you the answers and all about it, right now. Boom, Boom. Having this kind of a guide, you start to appreciate what the Ancient Spiritual Teaching is all about. You can appreciate what the Spirit has to teach us. It fills out our life and makes it whole. That is why I feel so excited about being able to talk about Travel by Soul, because Travel by Soul is the guts, the heart and the bottom line of this whole experience.

If you don't get the Travel by Soul bit, what have you got? You have just another religion. Religions are not good for our purpose. Religions control people as a social program. God created us as individuals. Let us start acting and thinking and being an individual. Accept the training down the pipeline through you to your outer environment. And that is what this thing is all about! I get quite excited when I talk about Travel by Soul and I feel this very vitally and strongly. Travel by Soul is so wonderful to me that I can't separate feeling from my experience with IT. The Truth is unique and very comforting.

Earlier in this book we talked about setting goals and now I think we might emphasize it again. When you are going to Travel by Soul, you have to have an objective. You cannot just pop off and Travel by Soul. Where are you going in your travels? What are you going to do? Where are you going to go? What do you expect to do when you get there? There is no objectivity unless you do this. You have to direct and concentrate your energies on something to make it become real for you. That is why we talked about forming objectives or goals. We used the word goal instead of objective, but these words have the same meaning. When you set a goal, your energies are concentrated on a particular thing.

When I go to bed at night or I set myself up for an experience, - I sit there or lay there and establish a goal. I determine that I need to know this, this, and this. I have to become more aware of this, this, or this. Whatever it is, that I feel I need to know - at this point I have some questions and I need the information. It is given to me.

An example of this type of thing happened when I was preparing some material to present in these

discussions. I thought I needed to know about the
subject of Consciousness. Well, when I woke up the
next morning, I had the whole story on Creation
instead of Consciousness! So, I picked myself up and
asked myself another question. Maybe I was mistaken
and maybe I really needed to know about Creation
after all. Or, just maybe Consciousness is Creation.
Well, I have learned never to doubt the function of
the Spirit or the Supreme Deity Consciousness
(remember?). I accepted what had been given to me and
I went to the table with my pad of paper and pen and
wrote it all down. So here it is - the story of
Creation.

When I get this kind of insight, a message to
solve my problem, or an understanding, it tells me
that I am doing something right. I am doing things
to get results. I am causing something to happen
spiritually. It is a pay day! When I come up blank,
then I have something I need to work on. I have a
problem - I have to do something different. I have
to investigate this part of myself and become
self-conscious of it. I need to get involved so I
identify with it personally or Beingly or some how
take it into my BEING. When this happens, the answer
is given to me, sometimes in strange ways.

Maybe Consciousness is Creation. Maybe there is
some relation we should look at. Do you think they
are one and the same thing? We have each been told
in various ways that all the lower worlds on the

Spiritual Worlds of Chart 1 was what was created.
This is the same creation described in the Christian
Bible book of Genesis. These stories tell us how
things were created; when it was created, etc. We
will not belabor what was said but that is the type
of creation we are talking about, in the lower four
levels of the spiritual world chart.

So I ask you the question now - What was created?
If it is like what we have been taught previously in
the past it was the creation of worlds, and universes
and the heavens above and the earth below, etc. But
this does not give me anything I can grasp or
understand. I don't know what they were writing
about. I do know that if we are going to understand
creation we have to ask more questions. I know I'm
not on target because I am not getting the answers,
right?

We might ask questions like this:
Did God create things?
Did God create toys?
Did God create automobiles?
Did God create how we live?
Did God create husbands and wives and children?
Did God create the relationship of husbands,
   wives and children?
Did God create nations, worlds and universes? No. No?
Did God create Souls? YES.

O.K. There has to be some difference between the creation of Soul and these other things we mentioned. That is part of your problem, understanding what consciousness is. We have to understand what it was that was created.

What was created had to be available to each and every person or Soul, didn't it? Everyone had to have it. So it could be available to you. Do you agree? What was created had to be attainable to each and every person or Soul if he reached out for it and tried to get it. Is that true? Can you accept that?

Whatever God created had to be usable. It had to provide a function or be created for a purpose. Can you accept that? Whatever was created had to be adaptable or changeable. Is that right? Can you each accept that? Change is the biggest thing with which we have to contend. Change, change, change, everything is changing constantly. Why? That is what we are going to understand here in a few minutes, if you don't already.

Why are things changing? We know that each individual or Soul who uses this creation stuff makes an individual application of it, doesn't he? The individual Soul changed it from what it was when somebody else used it, or when somebody else experienced it. This thing is all wrapped up into a big ball. We can put our arms around this Thing. This is getting to be fun. You can change the Thing

for your need, for your evolvement, for your
development wherever you are. Isn't that kind of
wonderful? Now stop and think about that. That has
to be a great point of our understanding.

In our previous discussion we were talking about
what was real and our awareness of reality. Remember
we said that whatever was real had to exist?
Remember that? And when we use our spiritual senses
and saw the Boxer dog lying on the floor, that was
real. And the dog does exist somewhere. This fact
that creativity exists, that creation exists is
something real and tangible that we can grab hold of
and start enjoying it. All things that exist must be
real and the reality of it must be with each Soul.

We were discussing that on the Chart 2 where
reality appears to Soul. So, everything that is
created has to have a reality for Soul. Now here is
the Big Heavyweight: That is that above all else,
creativity had to provide the training, it had to
provide the purification, it had to provide the
evolvement of each Soul to return back to the
Godhead, the Supreme Deity!! There is no reason to
create anything if it was not created to help us do
that.

If we are truly Soul and not this old bunch of
bones and rags, and if our identity is truly Soul,
then Soul must return sometime, somehow, some way to
its origin. That is a real strong statement, because
that is what the Ancient Spiritual Teaching does. It

gets us on the path. We start a spiritual opening up or this evolvement. The Ancient Spiritual Teaching shows us the way to experience and to cause this return. And as we proceed along in our outward and inward initiations, it means that we have attained a certain ability, talent, certain performance to attain the initiation.

It is nice to know that we have an initiation to record our evolvement because people need a feeling that they are not slipping backward; that they are not drifting aimlessly; that they are making some progress. We need some kind of a yardstick to measure what we are doing. I used to ask questions of rabbis, priests, and ministers, "What kind of yardstick do you use to know what kind of spiritual progress you are making"? They just got indignant. That kind of thinking really irritates them. They don't want to have any question like that put to them. Then I would ask, "How many Souls do you save each day, each week, or each month? How many Souls have you saved during the last year"? Souls? They don't use the word hardly at all. They don't know about this kind of stuff. They don't think about it. They are not trained to do this. Because they are working in the Kal and in the negative area. These people worship negative Gods and they are not tuned into this kind of thinking.

We have been learning some of the tools and the things that we need to use to experience Travel by

Soul, and these are the very things that we need to keep us moving along the path up towards the Godhead, our origin. Sri Paul Twitchell says that you cannot do it any other way. When he says there is no other way, that is pretty important to me. It is something that I have to work on and say to myself if there is no other way then I had better learn all I can as quickly as I can, all about it. I have to learn this creative approach towards Travel by Soul and evolvement, to attain my ultimate goal.

To enter the reality of Soul, creation had to enter Soul's consciousness shown on our Chart 2. Our mental consciousness is in the mind area and we become aware of things with the mind. As long as we are on this physical plane and in our physical body, regardless of what we do with Soul experience, we always have to come back and be aware of it in our mind. This is where we are and Sri Paul says that as long as we are here, we can't refute it, we have to stay here and work it out, live it out. So we have to do that.

All spiritual experience, then, comes back to the mind, back to the mental mind awareness. So when you have a dream and you come back to the awake stage again and you have complete memory of what the dream was and you know all about it, give yourself a little pat on the back, you are doing things right. You are succeeding! At the time when you have learned to control your dream through questions, the awareness will happen. I know, it happens to me.

Controlling your dreams is one of the ways to make the spiritual experience work. The dream is a thing you have right in your hands almost. The dream is yours to begin with and is personal and when you are in control of your dream the vagueness of the dream will develop into a full spiritual experience for you. When you can control your dreams, then you can work on Travel by Soul positively. We don't want to discuss dreams; however, I have found this principle is not well understood and is not discussed much in dream classes. The people leading the classes haven't understood this either. We need to relate these things together and orient them in our lives. So when you have a dream / Travel by Soul experience, it comes across from Soul to mind on our Chart 2 and you are aware of it.

Several years ago I found myself putting two words together and they seem to fit together. The words are conscious awareness. These two words seemed to fit six or seven years ago before I had the full understanding of them that I do today. Creativity is part of consciousness and if I am not aware of what was created, I have not gone very far. All this stuff is going to come back to mind and you have to develop in your mental abilities the ability to accept and receive that kind of awareness.

You have to discipline your mind so that it doesn't cancel it out, push it aside, or get the mental functions in there again. You have to discipline your mind to accept it. This concept is not compatible with the mind - as all prior training permitted the mind to rehash and recycle memory, and the earthly things. The earth oriented mind must recognize there is a Creator there, that there is a Deity or Being that regulates my life and I have to recognize it. When you get to that point, then awareness starts to show through.

We use the tools and techniques as building blocks to keep moving along, building us up and going ahead. We can enter into all the states of consciousness by placing the thought or idea of our Soul into Being, and that is what we have been doing here. The reality of it that exists on the physical plane manifests for us. Whatever we desire can be formed into absolute experiences of that conscious item of creation. We have established the consciousness of what was created, or a part of it, which is our state of consciousness.

Let us agree now on what was created.

There is a consciousness for everything that is created. We now have a consciousness of the toys; a consciousness of the airplanes; of the social order; a consciousness of everything. So everything is a consciousness. God didn't create worlds or universes

or heavens and earth - God created the consciousness
of those things. That is where we are - what we have
to do now is to ask ourselves how this relates to you
and me.

If everything was created as a consciousness and I
as Soul pick off a little piece. I bite off the
apple, take a chunk of it into my Soul, what
happens? The bite I take isn't the same as you take,
even if we took it off the same apple, is it? Each
of us takes his own bite. Each of us chews the bite
in a different way? Some of us swallow and some of
us spit it out. So it is not the same thing is it?
The origin is the same. The consciousness is there
and for a way of explaining this in the English
language, we say it is a state of consciousness.

You have a state of consciousness of that real
existence and I have a state of consciousness of the
same reality of existence. We each individually have
our own state of consciousness of that reality. So
we have an interesting situation. When the living
Spiritual Master said in his book Winds of Change
that everything was changing, Sri Harold was not
necessarily speaking from the viewpoint of Travel by
Soul, but was writing to people who were going to
read the book without any knowledge of Travel by Soul
yet. What he is saying, is that there has to be an
application to you through the inner Being, the inner
intelligence and instruction. Sri Harold is saying
that everything is undergoing change and is

changeable. We each took the little piece of creation and we recreated it in our own form, so we could use it to develop our own evolvement on the path upward.

This is important because when we took this thought across from Soul and gave it form, it became a thought form. After mind had materialized or made it manifest in our environment, the five senses said, yes, Uh Huh, that is right. I see it - I feel it - I taste it, and the mental awareness said it is there so it is real. You are aware of the reality of it.

So, if you took this little bite of creation and chewed it, swallowed it, digested it, and it became a part of your Being; then you have established a state of consciousness. You created it. You made it manifest in the physical world experience. You caused it. You were the cause in the Cause and Effect relationship which is the spiritual law which governs the lower physical worlds. You brought it into being. O.K. now this is important because the state of consciousness is different for each of us.

Soul is challenged to have those spiritual experiences which will provide the means for Soul's return back to the Godhead, its origin. We have to have these experiences. We have to experience things through imaging and Travel by Soul in order to make this progress and this return. Soul is purified through the experience, purified though the experiencing and its conscious awareness that

81

exists. When we speak of conscious awareness we are
talking about everything on the Soul side of Chart
II. We are talking about the consciousness of
creativity, what is created and we get an awareness
of that consciousness. This is the whole thing
wrapped up in a nut shell, if we do that.

Unless we get ourselves in the right position to
receive the Travel by Soul experience, I have found
that it doesn't happen. I have been saying this over
and over until it sounds like a broken record, but
believe me I say it because it is what I know to be.
I really think that most people that have trouble
with the Travel by Soul experience just are not doing
these things, they are not making it happen. You set
the stage and then you relax and sit back and enjoy
the play, so to speak.

During each of our lives, we have questions
regarding our relationship with other people or
Souls. Like what do you do if you are close to an
alcoholic or what happens during a divorce of two
people? Remember, the people or your relationship to
the person was not created by God. The consciousness
of it was created. The consciousness within each
Soul was created and that is what you have to work
with. Using your communication skills to share the
consciousness you desire with another person should
allow each person to become coordinated.

You can establish similar goals and objectives.
In the case of a divorce, there is an obvious absence

of consciousness or goals needed to be compatible. If a loved one has a habit such as smoking and alcohol and that person refuses to give up the habit, there is very little you can do for them until they become aware and they are willing to allow the consciousness to enter their Being. This is quite similar to membership in the Ancient Spiritual Teaching. Until you are ready on the inner planes you cannot be on the path or stay on the path of this teaching. These things are relative of course and success depends on many things such as the strength of love between two Souls, the ability of one to prepare the state of consciousness for sharing with the other, etc. Each Soul has its own reality.

Down through the evolution of Soul, Soul has come through the Gold Yuga, the Silver Yuga, the Copper Yuga and is now in the Iron Yuga of time. The Soul has developed and increased its awareness as it progressed to this current physical life. Some have progressed faster or slower than others as we each have our individual awareness and reality. When a person or Soul is ready to accept a new consciousness, then they can receive the consciousness so that you know where you are going (this nice knowing feeling), what you want to do with yourself, then the lower consciousness will not harm you. You are not going to change anything. You are not going to change another person. You are not going to stop the drinking or the smoking. You won't

change their attitude on anything. But God the
Supreme Deity will, if it is right and proper for
that person. And, by not placing yourself in
judgement of the person yourself, you are not
creating negative karma for yourself. You do not
allow yourself to be pulled into the consciousness
where you can be affected by it.

As an individual, we have extreme difficulty
getting ourself on the path and staying in the middle
of the path. You as an individual create a state of
consciousness, only for yourself, and no one else.
You can communicate to another Soul only those things
that the other Soul is ready to accept. We will
discuss the Spiritual group consciousness as a part
of "Holograms of Soul" later in this book and see how
we communicate from Soul to Soul.

Have you been trying to image your thoughts? A
chela has said that he is experiencing a lot of
insects like spiders and wonders what he can do about
them. Now, you have created these spiders haven't
you? So if you created them you can remove them or
destroy them can't you? If you don't want spiders in
your consciousness, then eliminate the spider
consciousness. Get rid of it, get them out of your
life.

I will share an experience I had with mosquitoes.

I was at a gold and silver mine on the

hot summer night. I was in my bunk with a light sheet over me. The mosquitoes were causing all kinds of torment, buzzing around me. I was getting all upset because they were zeroing in and divebombing on me and I was getting welts on my body whether they stung me or not. So I finally got myself under control and started disciplining myself. I said to myself, "Well, I created these mosquitoes, I brought them into the cabin with me so we could be together and if I don't like the mosquitoes, that is my problem." So, my thought process went like this. The mosquitoes are here and if they want to sting me, that is what it has to do to survive. Biting is part of his thing and it has to suck a little blood once in the life cycle to survive.

Since I created these mosquitoes, I'll just let them bite. I threw back the sheet from my body and let them bite all they wanted. I determined that they would not hurt me since I had created them. I am responsible for what I create. I soon got sleepy and fell off to sleep. The next morning, I didn't have any bites. There wasn't a single bite on my body! When you do this

remember, you just cannot say NO. That is
not enough. Rejection of anything is a
negative. That is not good enough. You
have to put something positive in there -
to replace the undesired thought of bites
with a good or acceptable thought. You
can't create a vacuum in space; you just
can't take something out of space and
have nothing there. I accepted a bunch
of friendly mosquitoes that weren't going
to harm me, that weren't going to bite.
It never did happen.

It is so important that we each learn to image our
thoughts, that we will work through one more
example.

A chela states that she has a desire
for a motor bike. After many questions
we found she imaged it like this. She
thinks she would like a good bike that
has everything good on it. It has a 250
or 300 cc engine and is a Kawasaki or a
BMW. The color is blue and brown. Blue
is on the fuel tank with brown trim. It
has some chrome and yellow with the
chrome on the sprocket, chain and wheel
rims and spokes and handlebars. The seat

is soft an cushy.

See what you have imaged? What else do you have
to do to make it materialize? You already have the
desire for it. Do you have a place to buy it? You
know where a dealer is selling bikes on Main Street.
What are the ways that people usually buy things when
they don't have money? They get credit. They get a
loan on a credit program, or a gift. See what is
happening to the image? You also need to be able to
drive the bike and you need a driver's license. A
plan might be necessary to prepare for the event in
the future. And if so, each item on the plan is
brought up to the present moment of time as it is
scheduled and the small items on the plan materialize
as you go along, until the whole motor bike exists.

CHAPTER 5

HOLOGRAMS OF SOUL

I had been Traveling by Soul or having out-of-body
experiences many years before I was given the
complete understanding of the HOWS and WHYS that
bring it about. I wanted to be able to Travel by
Soul at any time or all the time or at least be able
to control the experience with my needs as determined
through Soul. During the years of 1978 and 1979 the
rest of the jigsaw puzzle was revealed to me.
    I was employed by the Boeing Aerospace Company in
Kent, Washington at this time. To get away from the
demands of the job, I started spending my noon lunch
break in the cab of my pick-up truck in the Boeing
parking lot. I started out in the usual spiritual
exercise stance or procedure which soon changed into
a continual flow of the Spirit. I found that my mind
or brain was disciplined in technical fields of
science and that I could program my mind to be
receptive.
    I carried to the truck a tablet of paper and a
pen. Things were revealed to me and I wrote them
down on my paper. The next day I would reread what I
had been given the previous day and I found that I
was up to speed and could start where I had stopped
without any preliminary procedure. It prevented
lapses or discontinuity and it took on the aspects of

a continual revelation. This was great and I knew I was getting the Spirit flow that I needed.

Each person is an individual and my mind (the engineering mind) functions using outline form and that is the way the information came to me. I would outline my inputs on a tablet of paper and the Knowing of it was given to me to fill in all the details. Outlining allowed me to keep up with the rampant wild input I was receiving. This information on Holograms of Soul is the story given to me during a three month period followed by the ensuing years of refinement of my application and understanding.

When we know ourself and gain a self-knowledge of how we relate to the state of consciousness we exist in, and we learn to become a channel for the Spirit (Word), we can obtain everything we desire. We must know the consciousness of our self to approach and enter into Spirit itself. When we are free of all negativeness, we are allowed by Spirit to become a distributing channel which produces forms in this world. That is a very key thing because the first sentence read says by self-knowledge and becoming a channel for the Spiritual flow, we will make progress toward the altar of Spirit.

I am going to show you how you can do that. The body or mind itself does not have the power to see or perceive any external object. Your eyes do not perceive anything in your external world. Soul is the originator of all thoughts. The mind does not

think as we have been taught all our lives. We have
shown that consciousness was what was created and
that establishes the universes, which in turn has its
origin in an idea in thought and it has its
completion in the manifestation of the thought form.
There are many intermediate stages that are necessary
but the series of the cause and effect are the
thought and the thing.

I am here to discuss what these intermediate steps
are so that you can do it. We must first consider a
new force we will call the power of feeling. The
thought creates form, but it is feeling that gives
energy or vitality to the thought. I have
contemplated on this concept for many years and it
has taken a long time to understand it.

Now to go back a long time to build up to what we
want to talk about. When I was a small child, four
or five years old, I observed that a lot of things
were happening around me that I didn't even know
about; I could not perceive, I could not understand.
I knew that my dog could hear sounds I could not
hear. My dog could sense things I could not sense.
I knew that birds could sing songs and make notes I
could not hear. I knew that the little spiders that
hatch out in the spring time, with a brain of such
infinitesimal size that you can't even see it, knew
how to spin their intricate web. Nobody was there to
tell them how to do this because the parents, the
male and female spiders, had both been killed in the

winter frost. They weren't around to teach the little spider how to spin a web or to make a spinneret so that the baby spider can fly through the air for miles and miles to transport itself around.

These things bothered me and I have worried about it all my life, until I found out what was going on. And frankly, I went through the University and graduated in Electrical Engineering and I still did not know. They don't teach you this kind of thing at the universities or schools and it was a long time in coming. I had my own ideas about what was going on and I knew there was some kind of divine guidance involved. I felt that somehow my human culture had been bypassed and I was not in the line to get this kind of direction. So that is where we come to the descriptive topic: HOLOGRAMS OF SOUL.

This is a phrase I have coined to express what we are going to talk about. The "Hologram of Soul" is the utilization of the Light and Sound energy of Soul to create form of the thought to manifest on the physical plane.

In order to do this, we have to learn how the eye really works. We have to make a communication of some kind with the group consciousness which we will call the Spiritual Group Consciousness. We are going to identify holograms and we are going to learn how to manifest form, for example, how do you make a booK appear on the desk or table. How do you create all those things in your environment? That is what we

are going to do. So if you are not excited by now,
well, I don't know what to do with you. Maybe we can
give you a free pass to a hockey game. I think this
subject is the most fantastic one you can spend your
time on!

Each of us has been exposed to our own physical
experiences and in the Ancient Spiritual Teaching we
learn that there are some other types of experiences
- namely, spiritual experiences. Throughout the
evolution of man, there has been a conflict between
divine guidance and what your physical senses tell
you. Down through history people have said, "Oh, I
believe what my senses tell me. If I heard it, I
believe it, it is correct." There are those people
who say that seeing is believing and they believe
everything their eyes tell them, and I don't know how
much you believe your eyes tell you.

I am going to show you a little sleight of hand
trick. I am going to hold a quarter coin in my left
hand between my thumb and forefinger. I will just
grab the coin with my right hand by wrapping around
the coin. When I raise my right hand and open it,
the coin has disappeared! Ha, Ha, that is how easy
it is to fool the eye. There are many magicians
fooling the public daily. You don't have to do
anything very difficult to fool the eyes. If you
think seeing is believing, you are misguided.

The senses of taste and smell are fooled by
artificial scents and perfumes. Hearing gets

confused in tones and directions. Let us go on a little bit and find out if we can establish what is really true, what is real. That is what Eckankar has given me. It has given me a sense of reality. Reality is a thing that, Boy, there is nothing like it. Obviously, our senses give us only illusions.

About seven years ago, the Seattle Science Center presented a display on holograms and for the first time the whole problem came together for me. It happened just like a big splash in a pond. It all fits together and the holograms were one thing that started me on an investigation that placed the answers together and made it jell. There are many kinds of holograms which satisfy many different functions. Holograms can provide the image which stands out in space away from the walls. These are a three-dimensional type and you can walk around on the back side of them and the other side. It is something fascinating to see. If you have an opportunity to visit a scientific display of holograms, please go and do so.

The cover of the National Geographic Magazine, March 1984, has a display that shows the three-dimensional picture. You can actually see behind the eagle's legs and under its wings have a nice feeling from it. That is what we are going to talk about and how the hologram is presented. I am going to explain a little bit about what the hologram is, but like it says in The Flute of God, the true

teacher does very little for you but to point the
way. I do not have time here to talk very much about
holograms or the scientific derivation of holograms.
I am not all that big an authority on the scientific
background myself. However, I want you to know there
is something that is there that is tangible and that
science recognizes as fact. If you want to find out
more about holograms, please go after it and find
out.

The hologram is first of all an image on a
photographic plate where the light is shattered by a
laser. The laser light continues through to a grid
and part of the light is reflected over at a 90
degree angle (see Chart 3). This grid is called a
diffraction grid. Maybe some of you have used this
type of grid in your physics class work in school.
The diffraction grid allows some light to pass
through and this light is reflected by a mirror over
to a point in space. The rest of the light is
reflected at right angles where it is spread or
magnified up to the size of the object. In this case
they use a chess man as the object to be imaged. The
light comes out at a point where it can be combined
with the other half of light to form the image in
space. This is the way science develops a laser
picture and the formation of the laser is very
important.

The laser is a highly concentrated pure coherent
light beam; that is, it does not have all the other

colors, only one. It is very pure and very single in
its makeup. When science makes a laser to form a
hologram, they use a crystal of a ruby to generate a
pure unadulterated light beam of the red frequency.
So they end up with a picture of just one color. I
am going to show you in a few minutes what happens in
Soul where God has made our eyes so that they are not
limited to one ruby red frequency. We have the whole
color spectrum available in the white light. So, we
can use any shade, hue or color that we want to enjoy
with our eyes.

We have to explore our own eyes so that we know
what we are working with. I have some diagrams shown
in Chart 4, Fig. (a). If you take a cardboard and
punch a fine hole in the middle of it, and if you
permit the image of an object to come through the
whole on a screen, you will see that the image is
reversed. The bottom becomes the top and the top
becomes the bottom. In the same way your eye messes
you up. Little children depend on their mother and
father to tell them what direction is up and down
until the brain learns this. The eye continually
sees things in the inverse position.

We need to know about cycles and vibration. In
Chart 4, Fig. (b), we will generate a cycle.
Starting at the center line we will call it zero and
go up in a positive direction and come back down to
zero and swing below the centerline to the negative
position and back to the point of origin. This is a

96

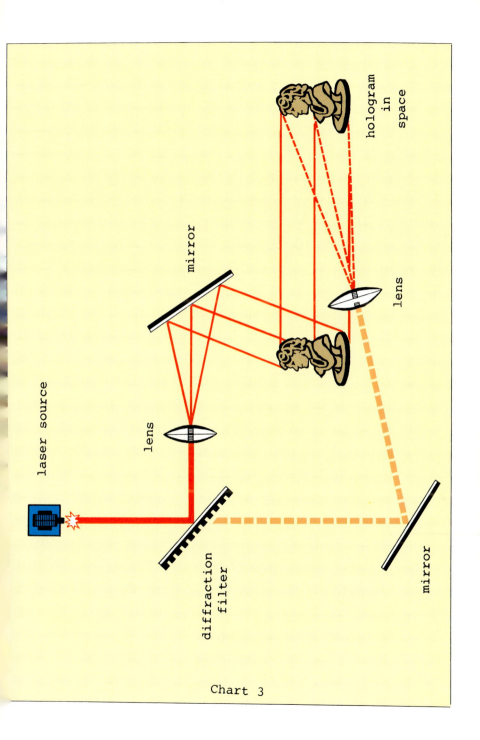

Chart 3

97

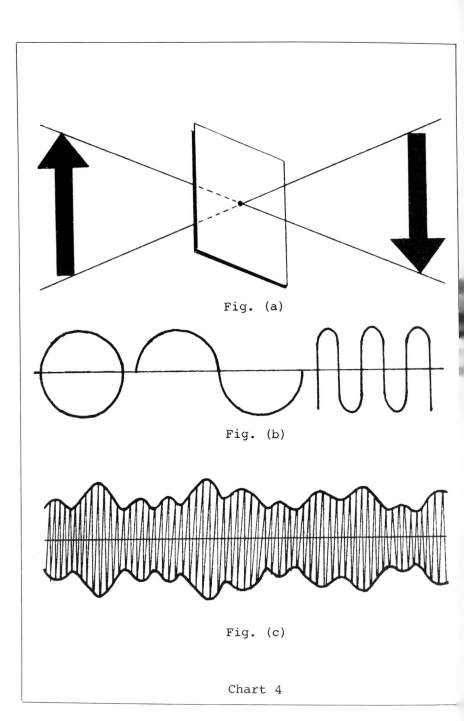

Fig. (a)

Fig. (b)

Fig. (c)

Chart 4

98

complete cycle. We call this a cycle. We learn in the Ancient Spiritual Teaching that all things we know or experience happens in cycles. Everything repeats and repeats in cycles. In Figure (b) of Chart 4, if you take the first half of the cycle and zip up through the positive half and come down to the centerline but instead of returning to the point of origin, move it out along the centerline you can give it some longitudinal acceleration so that it moves out into space.

Visualize this as when you drop a pebble into a pond, the waves move out from the center. You now have longitudinal motion and forward motion, so the cycle moves over a displacement of that much. The complete cycle is called a period of the vibration. There are many kinds of vibrations and we very seldom find one that is in the pure state in nature. Vibrations combine and form combinations of vibations.

Another part of the puzzle that I have to resolve was the statement I had heard in the Ancient Spiritual Teaching, "as it is above, so it is below." As it is in the spiritual world, so it is in the physical world. I didn't quite understand how this is possible. Things that exist up in the spiritual areas I am supposed to be able to hear, or smell or taste down on the physical; but it is due to the vibratory affair.

When I was in grade school and high school we had

small super heterodyne radios that were the ac-dc radios of our youth. I think the super heterodyne has been replaced by the solid state transistor radios of today, but that is where it started. The concept of the super heterodyne was that the high frequency vibration was combined with another high frequency and at those places where they were both positive they were additive and those places where they were both negative and positive they were subtractive; the rest of the combined frequency vibration fell in between those two extremes.

This provided an intermediate frequency which was very low in vibration rate. It was sometimes called the beat frequency which was very low in vibration rate. It was sometimes called the beat frequency because it was the result of the two frequencies beating against each other. In Chart 4, Fig. (c), the intermediate beat frequency was then varied in amplitude by the voice or music and this made the radio or T.V. sound. We are talking about reducing kilo-cycles down to one cycle or mega-cycles down to one cycle or going from one million down to one cycle. So now this is how the vibratory rate changes from the spiritual worlds to the physical world so that our slowed down senses can perceive on this level.

The day this phenomenon was revealed to me, I was driving my pick-up home after work. As I stopped at a traffic light my engine RPM meshed with the RPM of

100

a truck stopped beside me. The vibration rates of our two engines was slowed down so low that it was just a throbbing low frequency. Amazing!

Now let us talk about the eye. The eye is an interesting physical organ. I show some drawings of eyeballs in Chart 5. In Figure (d), the eye has a lens in front and the retina in the back with the optic nerve shown. You will notice that the lens is similar to the surface of a mirror. The concave surface on the inside surface and a convex surface on the outside. The lens collects the light image and focuses it on the retina on the back of the eyeball. The lining of the eyeball is covered with the retina which is similar to the photographic plate of the hologram about which we have been talking.

Chart 5, Fig. (d), #1 shows the lens focusing on the retina which would make it a healthy normal eye. The eye shown in Figure (d), #2 shows the lens focusing beyond the retina and it is called a far sighted eye and is out of focus and provides blurred vision. Figure (d), # 3 shows an eye that focuses in front of the retina and is also out of focus and is referred to as a near sighted eye, and provides blurred vision. The complete eyeball is shown in Figure (e) with the optic nerve at the back of the eyeball. This eye can focus on any point on the retina that is chooses. The muscles can contract or expand the eyeball to vary the focal point on the retina and selects any point desired.

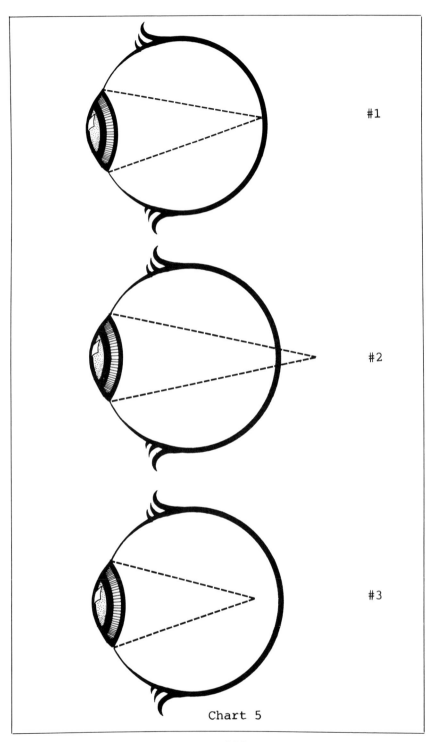

#1

#2

#3

Chart 5

102

What is happening here is another thing that is
not taught in school books. I have proven to myself
that it works. All the information that comes to us
comes through Soul and we bring that thought down
from the spiritual planes, down to the mental plane
where the mind mulls around with it a little bit and
says, "this seems like a good thing to do." Mind
determines that it should try this one and see how it
works. So, in the subconscious part of the brain
determines that it is going to use this thought. The
thought is given form on the Causal Plane and it is
given the emotional expression and feeling on the
Astral Plane then it is sent to the eye where it is
placed on the retina as a point source of light.

The eye is told to look for a certain image and it
scans the surface of the retina until it finds it.
Sometimes it has difficulty locating the image Soul
wants mind to look at and so other things happen.
Due to the karmic influence, or the experiences
recorded by the mind, or the emotional aspects
assigned to the thought on the Astral Plane were not
proper, etc., the image does not show up. Then we
see other related things or whatever mind throws in
there for us to see. We see it differently than what
is true or pure!

The mind can give us the flash insight we were
taking about before. Mind can give us illusionary
vision of its choosing in the place of the Hologram
of Soul it was instructed to show. When the mind is

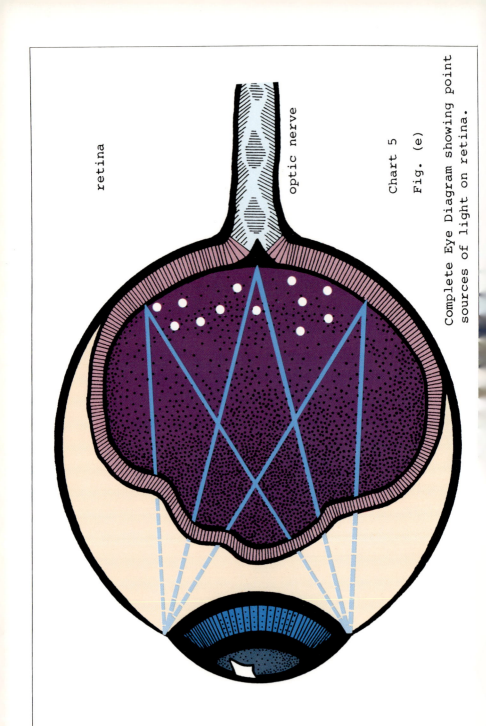

retina

optic nerve

Chart 5

Fig. (e)

Complete Eye Diagram showing point
sources of light on retina.

not trained or disciplined it can show whatever it wants to show. When Soul has established a goal or objective and the energy of the light and sound within Soul is concentrated to form the image and Soul forces mind to bring this image into the present moment of time, mind is forced to locate it on the retina. This is why we say it is so important to place your attention on what you want to do.

When the eye focuses on the image the Hologram of Soul has placed on the retina, the eyeball adjusts to do the job of projecting that image out into the environment of that person. The outer lens must focus for the wavelength and focal point required for the image to exist in space. When the image or hologram is to be nearby the human body, some of the other senses can be brought in to verify the taste, the smell, the feel and the hearing of sounds to establish in the mind that it actually does exist - it is real, which is relayed to the Soul as the awareness of that existence.

The scientific community has established a phenomenon which is 180 degrees in the other direction. They cannot find the truth or purity in their outer environments because they have eliminated the basic relationship to truth and purity - namely the link to Spirit and God!! There is no way that the very happenings of which science deals with can be random, haphazard and without direction or purpose! God, through Spirit provides purpose and reason for

105

everything in creation. Therefore, it follows in
logic (a function of the scientific mind) that all
those things in the environment with which science
deals, must come from within.

To expect such happenings to occur in the outer
worlds of environment without divine guidance, order
and systematic arrangements is preposterous! The
scientific method of analysis and solving problems is
based on and requires the happenings to be orderly
and systematic and predictable! Applications of
virtually millions of applied phenomena use the
concept of controlled, directed search schemes,
chemistry, for example, to detect those happenings.
Those very happenings searched for can be found and
identified because of their systematic order and
predictability which do not exist in the outer
environment of the individual's emotions and
feelings.

I would like to carry the idea of vibration a step
further and we will talk about some heady things that
scientists like Dr. Einstein and Dr. Compton and
others have given to us. We will talk about the
Quantum Theory. The Quantum Theory states that all
light is composed of radiation of the units of
radiation called photons. The photon is the thing we
use to measure the amount of light that is radiated.
Each photon is identified depending upon the amount
of energy it contains, which in turn is determined by
its wavelength. The amount of energy this photon

carries is directly proportional to its wavelength.
The energy that any object can absorb when it comes in contact with light is based upon the frequency of the vibration of the wavelength of that photon. When an object like your body gets in the way of a light radiation, your body absorbs that light, that energy. The ability of your body to absorb light radiation is determined by the vibratory rate the body is attuned to receive by Soul. The Body Aura Indicator of vibratory rate of a body is established in the body aura around that body. They can be additive or subtractive and cancel each other out forming holes or discoloration in the aura. The interaction between Soul and mind will determine how your body is programmed to absorb light energy.

You can not afford to sit there like a wart on a pickle and just let the world go by. As people and as Spiritual Students we are challenged, we are exhorted, we are encouraged to do whatever is necessary to get off our butts and get going. We have to do things for ourselves. We can recreate everything God has created in our environment. You must establish what your body energy level is to be by the use of the Hologram of Soul you project through your body aura and into your environment. You can determine if your body is to be well or sick with disease. You can create the whole smear!

When you are able to heal your body of a physical problem or disease, the healing is accomplished spiritually at this level. The absorbed energy level is regulated by the Holograms of Soul to bring into existence the proper attitudes, feelings and objectivity which manifests in the NOW OF TIME.

We have mentioned before that the mind comes between our physical Being and Soul. The brain is the limiting thing that prevents us from becoming God-like or doing those things God would like us to do. Limitations of the mind are very important because we can't do much until we get the mind straightened out. As long as we persist in ignoring why we are here in this life, in this place, wearing the clothes we are wearing, sitting in that chair, your mind will continue to distort everything in your Being.

We are going to discuss Chart 2. What happens, now, when you as an individual bring a thought down from Soul down to the mind. If it decided to assign it a form and gave it emotional aspects and to have it come into our present moment of experience - then I would like to suggest to you that the brain sends a message on the optic nerve and says to the eye, that over at some point on the retina there is an image. The eye is a trained eye and it has all these tiny little muscles controlling the eyeball tension and they can expand it or collapse it to make it focus on the retina at that one little pin point of image of light. There it sees the image the mind told it to look for.

We have each had flashing thoughts, where
something comes into our vision that we did not
expect - so we look at it anyway. The eye may look
at several images and selects one to put its
attention on. Now we put our attention on what the
mind has told it to look at and we concentrate on
this point, this image, that is on this point source
of light. The gray gelatinous fluid that fills the
eyeball provides the filtering function which slows
down the vibration rate and makes it so that it is
visible to the outer eye.

At this point, I would like to suggest that we
think about states of consciousness. We have already
discussed states of consciousness in detail, but we
need to relate the Hologram of Soul to the state of
consciousness. I know that you cannot learn or
understand Travel by Soul unless you understand what
the state of consciousness is and how you get from
one state of consciousness to another. I have given
you some of the tools I have used to get myself into
these states of consciousness.

Now, the time that your mind is seeing what it is
told to see, remember, that we more or less accept
the doctrine that all creation in the lower worlds is
complete; that everything that should have been
created is created; and that it exists in the
consciousness. So what we are talking about here is
that we are saying that whatever thought comes down
to mind, we ought to look at it. Mind can find it.

It exists and there are millions and jillions of
point sources of light that can contain the image
that is sent from Soul. All of creation exists some
place in the Light and Sound at a point source of
light on the retina!

The Holograms of Soul are not limited to one ruby
red laser frequency as the scientific hologram is.
The Divine Light contains all the color frequencies
in the rainbow ... The white light is available to
the eye as provided by Soul to see the image of its
desire. So you can revel in all the beauty of color
and hue and tint you wish to have

When the eye is told to project the conscious
image of a radio antenna pointer that I am using
during the discussion group talks, your eye projects
it for you. I had recreated the consciousness of it
and communicated the Spiritual Group Consciousness of
it to you and you also recreated your awareness of its
existence. We both see and enjoy the same consciousness
the same point source of light at the present moment.

Remember, there is a consciousness for everything
that was created. By using Holograms of Soul to
establish what we place our attention on, we bring our
Being into that state of consciousness and it is real
to us. It is a pure state of consciousness which
originated in Soul. The freedom to move from one state
of consciousness to another state of consciousness is
accomplished by Soul in this way. We call it Traveling
by Soul.

CHAPTER 6

CREATIVITY OF A SOUL FOR A SINGLE SOUL'S ENVIRONMENT

We will now discuss Table 1. At the top of the page it says that the basic concept is that everything in your worldly environment was created by you. You caused it to exist and only you are responsible for its creation. Now you have to think about that a lot to realize you can't blame your preacher, your minister, you can't blame your coach, you can't blame your teacher for any of it. You can't blame God - that is for darn sure! Soul has been given the freedom of choice and if you don't like what is happening to you, you can choose to do something different. You have created it and it is your responsibility.

Let us go to Table 1, Type one. Type one is the single Soul's environment. Items a. through f. are a review of what we have been discussing. Items 1 through 5 areas where you can practice what we have been discussing. You will find that you probably cannot do these things immediately, I have been working on it for many years. But you can do it enough times to get the thrill of it - and once you get going, it will jab you and prod you until you can't quit. You will just have to keep imaging everything.

The first item suggested for you to practice on is

TABLE 1

The basic concept is that everything in your worldly environment was created by you. You caused it to exist and only you are responsible for its creation.

TYPE 1   <u>CREATIVITY OF A SINGLE SOUL FOR A</u>
<u>SINGLE SOUL'S ENVIRONMENT</u>

a. Soul develops a thought; it is sent to the mind.
b. The thought is passed from the mental plane to the causal plane where it is assigned a form for its expression.
c. The <u>thought</u> <u>form</u> is then sent to the astral plane where it takes on emotional aspects of energy.
d. The thought form is then passed down to the physical earth plane where it is manifest.
e. The physical object is verified to exist by the five senses as Real.
f. This is instantaneous, of the present moment.

--Assume responsibility for your creation.

PRACTICE AREAS ...
1. Control your physical health.
2. Find lost items.
3. Control the weather.
4. Control events - make things happen, bring things into being.
5. Control birds, insects, animals.

REMEMBER - You are trying to bring an idea down into your mental awareness. To do this, make audible statements to yourself. Speak out loud and affirm what you believe to be. Write notes. Sing or do anything to impress your mind that it is so. Above all - be H-A-P-P-Y !!

TABLE 1 (cont.)

TYPE 2 CREATIVITY OF A SOUL INVOLVING OTHER SOUL'S ENVIRONMENT

g. This is more difficult; thought forms are communicated from your soul to other souls.
h. Simple communications involves the creativity process of TYPE 1 above (a. thru f.).
i. Use the expressive skills to give the thought form to another Soul (reading, writing, voice, feeling by touch, etc.).
j. For complex creativity - MAKE A PLAN (a list of events scheduled) to "PLAN YOUR WORK, THEN WORK YOUR PLAN." As time goes by, place attention on each element of the plan (bringing it from the past when the plan was made into the present moment giving it vitality and energy).
k. Your attention and the LIGHT AND SOUND energy brings each element into the present and it is materialized for you.

CAUTION - Do not cancel out or resist the plan once it is set in motion. To do so puts you in opposition to the Mahanta Consciousness and the Living Eck Master and nullifies all the good things done to help you create your plan. Do not leave a void or a vacuum - Always replace a bad idea with a better (different) idea. Change to an idea more satisfactory. The energy of the Master and all of the affected Souls will be on you. Disappointment, failure and frustration may prevail.

MAY THE BLESSINGS BE ...

the controlling of your physical health. There is
nothing that is more personal, or more direct, or all
encompassing than your own body. You and nobody else
can influence it.

So start out to control your body health. Heal
yourself. Purify yourself. Correct it so that it no
longer has disease. Look on your body as the
creation of Soul and Soul could not create anything
that wasn't perfect. Soul could not create anything
diseased. Soul could not create anything rotting or
decayed. Perfect Soul can't have any foulness or
dirtiness about perfect Soul - if you understand what
Soul is.

So if your Soul created your body it's got to be
perfect. You have to think of it in your mind with
mind's thirty-six symbols or digits as being
perfect. You have to tell yourself that you
understand there is no room for decay or rotting or
anything like that in this body that is manifest.
Perfection cannot exist with rot and decay.

You can have a lot of fun with this kind of thing
... I will share a couple of experiences I have had
with it.

When I lived in California, I had a
dentist who told me I had to come back to
have three cavities in my teeth fixed.
He had his sweet little assistant come in

114

and record it with red ink on the tooth
chart. She marked little X's in there
where the decays were. Well, this kind
of made me mad and I went home grumbling
about it. The Dentist was controlling my
consciousness and that irritated me. I
did not go along with that and I decided
I would not accept it.

So, I worked on myself for the two
weeks until my appointment time. When I
got to the dentist he opened my mouth and
looked at it. He looked back at his
chart and he looked back at my teeth
again. The doctor asked me, "Are you
sure I am supposed to find some decay in
your teeth?" I reminded him that he said
there were cavities and set the
appointment. He called in his assistant
and asked her, "Did you put these red
marks on this chart?" "Sure I did, that
was only two weeks ago and I remember
doing it." The doctor said that he could
not find them and he then took X-rays.
The doctor didn't find them on the X-rays
either. Soooo, I kept my money in my
pocket and walked away smiling!

This is the kind of fun you can have, and it is
really a game. It's a game with you and your

consciousness! If you can learn through your own experience all the wonderful things that you can have; the wonderful experiences you can have; the wonderful things you can do, then maybe you will get as excited as I am.

I have another experience which may help you understand how to control your health.

I was cutting and falling trees to clear a place to build a house on a wooded area. We removed eleven trees in all. These trees were large alders about fifteen to twenty inches in diameter. I had a stump that I was splitting and I had a wedge in the stump and a ten pound mall to hit it with. The mall raised above my head with arms extended was at least 300 to 400 foot-pounds of force which was adequate to split the wood. Well, this time, it glanced off the wedge and hit my foot. I had a light canvas shoe on and my foot was crushed. And I was in real agony. I was on the ground rolling around out there in the woods. I was holding my foot and writhing in pain, yelling and moaning and groaning and really feeling sorry for myself. Nobody was around to help me. My wife is a

trained nurse and if she had been there,
she would have lavished me with care.
But she wasn't there and after a while I
learned it was a blessing that she wasn't
there.

I don't want to discredit her ability
to comfort, but what she has learned in
medical training was to give physical
help and comfort. What I had learned in
the Ancient Spiritual Teaching was that I
didn't really need that. What I had to
do was to get myself some spiritual
comfort. I don't know how long I rolled
around on the ground because I was in
pain. By this time my foot was all
swelling up and misshaped. I had my
hands on it and it was mushing around in
my shoe and starting to swell up.

I started to tell myself what I
believed to be true. I started to tell
myself what my foot was like when it was
a perfect foot before it was hurt. You
have to be dramatic, you have to
verbalize these things so that your mind
- and I remind you it is limited to the
36 symbols, and you have to try things to
get its attention. You have to make an
impression on your mind. I was talking
to myself out loud what I had to do, what

117

my foot was supposed to be like, how it was supposed to be a perfect foot, I pictured it, I imaged it as the way I saw it before it was hurt. I refused to take my shoe off because that would verify the physical existence of an injury. I stayed there and lay on the ground on the pine needles until I got myself redirected.

Pretty soon, as soon as I started doing that, the pain began to leave and in a few more minutes the pain had disappeared completely. So I lay there five or ten more minutes - I don't know how long it was and soon I felt like I could sit up. I sat up and put a little weight on my heal. That felt pretty good and I kept talking to myself and forming images of a perfect beautifully shaped foot with nice pink color on the skin and everything in the right places. It might have a callous here or there but it was a good foot. I decided I was ready to stand and I got up and put a little weight on it and it felt good. After standing quietly for several more minutes, I started to walk around on it like before. I had a perfect foot again. I packed up my tools and went

home. I told no one about it until days
later. When I took my shower, I looked
at the wall while I washed my foot. I
didn't want to do anything which might
confirm an injury. My foot was perfect
again.

You can find lost items; you can control the
weather when everyone in our culture claims the
weather is uncontrollable. But you can control it
because it is a part of your environment.

One time when we had planned all week
to pay bills on a certain day, we turned
the rain on and off fourteen times in one
hour in Seattle. We had our small son
wrapped in blankets and we had lots of
stops to make. Every time we left the
car the rain would stop. When we got
into the store the rain started again and
it would just pour while we were in the
store. We would get ready to leave the
store and the rain would stop.

There are several attitudes that could be
discussed here. One is the attitude of following
through with the plan that had been made several days
prior. As we mentioned before, once you set a plan

in motion the Consciousness of the Inner Master gets
all other Souls' consciousness in line or in tune
with your objective - you must not violate that
energy. Another is you develop an attitude of
acceptance of God's work as you behold it. Things
are happening because it is to be. Things happen
with such regularity that you have to believe it.
Once you start an action in motion, you have to
accept the happening because it is so obvious to
you. You caused it. You made it exist. This is
wonderful!

I have used this Travel by Soul technique to visit
such places as the continent of Atlantis and the
continent of Lemuria or "MU" as it is called. These
civilizations existed long before recordation of
history, before the alluvial floods during the golden
yuga of time. This type of experience collapses time
and renders it useless. It was great to visit the
hot tropical jungles of the South Pacific and hot
muggy sweaty jungle smell and sensations.

Other areas suggested for practice on Table 1 are
the control of birds and animals and insects. These
are good ideas to practice on because each of us has
had some experience with them. Dogs are very sharp
and so eager to accept guidance from you, their
"master." Dogs still get the Divine Guidance we
talked about and that is fun to see working.

I have a good friend who has a boxer
dog named Max. Max is a watchdog and
guards his master's home and property
especially after dark. I had met Max and
we liked each other and I considered Max
to be my friend. I had arranged to
return a book to Max's master and it was
about nine o'clock in the evening. Since
it was dark I knew I would be confronted
by Max at the edge of the yard! When I
was a block from the house, I started
talking to Max to tell him I was coming
to visit him. I imaged his happy face
and I imaged my patting Max on the head
and we were friends. When I got there at
the house there was only quietness, not
growling or barking, etc. Max's master
was quite shaken that someone could
approach the house without Max sounding
the alarm. I explained to her that I had
talked to Max and he knew I was coming to
visit and he knew I was all right.

Table 1, Type 2 is Creativity of a Soul involving
another Soul's environment. The first steps are the
same as for the single Soul shown in Type 1. But now
we use the communicative skills or the expressive
skills to give this thought to another Soul. When I
hold up this object and tell you that this is my

121

pointer each of you see it. You say, "Yes, that is your pointer." We each put our attention on the pointer and it now exists in the reality of your consciousness. Sri Paul says that you experience what you put your attention on, and you'd better believe it. That is just what we are talking about here. You put your attention on that thing, bring it into the Now of Time and it gets the energy of the Light and Sound of the Hologram of Soul and it happens for you.

Table 1, Type 2, item j. is a complex situation where you make something happen in the future. In this part of it, I'm not telling you anything new but you make the plan or you formulate a plan. Go to an architect and tell him that you want to build a house. The architect listens to your ideas or images of how you want the floor plan and all that and he draws it the way he thought you explained it to him. When you see what he has drawn you say, "No, that is not what I had in mind. I want the kitchen door over here and the pots and pans stored over here, etc." The architect redraws your kitchen. He reimages it for you. This is the image of your house. What happens here is more complex than when you are doing it for your own Soul's environment in Type 1. There are many other Souls who each have their own environments to become effective. Something has to happen up here in the Spiritual planes shown in Chart 1.

The Consciousness of the Inner Master does it all for you. You are completely unaware of this and you don't even know it is happening, but it is being done. Now when you schedule it and put in some reference of time, one event comes before the other and each Soul has to act on it. The plumber has to get his act together and come in. The electrician has to come in and do his thing. The carpenter has to do something else and the roofer has to put on the roof. The banker had to finance the project, etc. It would never happen unless the Consciousness of the Inner Master was in there making it happen for you.

People have said to me that they get pretty discouraged and disappointed because everything seems to go wrong for them. Nothing works out for them. It is all bad. They blame "Fate" or somebody else for their failures. People do get discouraged when things don't work for them. First of all, whose fault is it? It is theirs, that person. Secondly, this plan you have set in motion is a horrendously big massive coordination of all the people (Souls) that are associated with the projects. If you violate the plan, you violate the Inner Master and all the energies concentrated to do it now spill over and you have a log jam. Those things in your world fall in on you and you have really goofed! But when you follow the plan each item or event materializes on time in its point in time and finally the house is completed. I have built three houses and remodelled another and I can tell you that it works when you learn what caused it!

CHAPTER 7

EXERCISES LEADING TO TRAVEL BY SOUL

Table 2 shows several exercises that will help you to do Traveling by Soul. The suggested way is to do a little at a time. You will find that some items are easier to do than others and some will take more time (weeks or months) to do. Contemplation is required to identify what you are doing and to make you aware of it.

Remember, the object is to gain as much self-knowledge of it (consciousness) as you can. So you have to ask all the questions you need to get full understanding.

When you have the self-knowledge and the complete understanding of that state of consciousness, then you have mastered it. The God Consciousness is the summation of all the little steps of mastership along the way. As you progress in your mastership of each state of consciousness, you will find that Soul is more fully in charge of your life and it gets easier as each new state of consciousness comes along.

One thing I have noticed is that the opportunity to experience a happening keeps returning to you until you do master it. The Kal will try to confuse and discourage you up to the point where you master it. Then it does not return any more! For example, when you heal yourself and make yourself healthy, the

TABLE 2

EXERCISES LEADING TO TRAVEL BY SOUL

1. REVIEW YOUR SPIRITUAL EXERCISE TECHNIQUES.

2. SET GOALS EACH DAY.

3. DEMONSTRATE HOW MIND AUTOMATICALLY IMAGES WHAT IT WANTS TO IMAGE.

4. CHANGE FROM SEEKING GOD (BESEECHING, PRAYER, EXPLOITING) TO SERVING GOD.

5. PRACTICE THE LAW OF CAUSE THE EFFECT.

6. EXPERIENCE REALITY USING THE SPIRITUAL SENSES.

7. PRACTICE BEING AWARE OF EACH IDEA AT THE MENTAL LEVELS - AT THE SPIRITUAL LEVELS.

8. IMAGE EACH IDEA
     TRY 3-DIMENSIONAL IMAGES (MOVE AROUND YOUR
         IMAGE AND SEE IT FROM DIFFERENT VIEWPOINTS).

9. IDENTIFY WHAT YOU KNOW (REALLY KNOW). IF TRUTH IS A KNOWING FOR YOU - EXPERIENCE TRUTH.

TABLE 2 (cont.)

10. IDENTIFY HOW FEELINGS CHANGE YOUR IMAGE OF IT.
MAKE A MOUNTAIN OUT OF A MOLE HILL.

11. IDENTIFY HOW YOUR ATTENTION ENERGIZES WHAT YOU
CONCENTRATE ON.

12. IDENTIFY HOW YOUR ATTITUDE ALTERS THE RESULTS.

13. IDENTIFY THE CONSCIOUSNESS THAT EXISTS FOR EACH
THING YOU HAVE AROUND YOUR EVERYDAY ENVIRONMENT.
BAKE A CAKE, MAKE A DRESS, BUILD FURNITURE,
REPAIR A CAR, ETC. GET YOURSELF LOST IN THE
PROJECT - BECOME ABSORBED IN THE CONSCIOUSNESS
OF IT.

14. VISUALIZE HOW YOUR STATE OF CONSCIOUSNESS CHANGES
- HOW IT DIFFERS FROM ANOTHER PERSON'S STATE OF
CONSCIOUSNESS.

15. BE AWARE OF HOW YOU CAN LEAVE ONE STATE OF
CONSCIOUSNESS AND ENTER ANOTHER STATE OF
CONSCIOUSNESS AND THEN RETURN TO THE FIRST STATE
OF CONSCIOUSNESS BY MOVING YOUR ATTENTION FROM
ONE TO THE OTHER.

Kal will recycle some other ailment or malady or pain and torment on you. You are again tested to see if you really have mastered it! Each time you master it, it gets easier to do and finally it is part of your Being. You are free of it.

Those exercises shown on Table 2 provide a review of the techniques we have been learning in this book. I would like to discuss some of them in more detail.

Item 8 suggests that we view things as a three-dimensional image when we think of them. This is different from how we are used to doing. We normally see things as the artist sees them, as a two-dimensional picture. I suggest that you develop the ability to see or image your thoughts as three-dimensional and try to go around on the other side of your image and see what it looks like on the back side of it. Instead of seeing things as triangles, see them as cone shaped, instead of seeing things as a square, see them as a cube, instead of seeing things as a circle see them as a sphere. In other words, see things as form occupying space.

In Item 13 of Table 2, try to identify your consciousness of each thing in your environment from the learning base of the mind. If we learn how it is here on earth in a physical environment, then we can relate it to the spiritual existance on other planes. For example, when you want a cake to exist in your environment, we have learned that certain

128

things must be done. We put our attention on the
thing we are thinking about. This directs the Light
and Sound energy on it. We bring the thought into
the Now of Time or the Presence of Time. Then we
proceed with visualizing the steps necessary to bring
it about.

Remember, the Sugmad did not create the cake, He
created the consciousness of the cake. So, when we
start to form the cake we do not have a cake. All we
start with is the flour, some spices and an egg or
two, etc. and a recipe. Whatever state of
consciousness we care to enter, we must follow or
work within the laws or rules of behavior for that
consciousness. So, when we are going to bake a cake,
we must conform to those rules of good kitchen
procedures and processes. O.K? We do what the rules
of good cake baking require. Not until we take it
out of the oven and get the frosting on it, is it a
cake. Then, the cake materializes as a cake. When
you decide to build furniture, you start out with
sticks of wood and glue and screws and tools, etc.,
you do not have a piece of furniture. The
consciousness of the furniture is what you have
because that is what was created. When you are
finished with the piece of furniture, it will look
different from other furniture because it is your
state of consciousness that you created and it is
your adaptation of the consciousness that God
created.

Art of Travel by Soul

When you are baking a cake or building furniture
or some other project like that, you become so
interested in what you are doing that you may lose
track of time or your surroundings. When you are
painting a picture, you might forget to stop in time
to wash up and cook your dinner. You are relating
yourself to the consciousness, and we call that self
consciousness. You have to relate your Being to the
consciousness to master it.

When your spouse of a friend calls you out of your
concentration and yells from the kitchen, "Dear,
would you come and fix the sink faucet, it won't shut
off?", your attention is changed from building
furniture to fixing the faucet and you put your
attention on the consciousness of the faucet. When
you have fixed the faucet, you go back to the shop
and place your attention on the furniture project
again. You have done these gymnastics on the
physical plane with the mind. The same routine is
done when we Travel by Soul. The only difference is
that we do it on the other planes within the
spiritual Being, to achieve Traveling by Soul.

Using the 36 symbol language to describe God, the
Supreme Deity, we say He is or has these
characteristics: He is omniscient or all Knowing, all
Knowledgeable, He is omnipresent or all present
everywhere at the same time, He is omnipotent or all
potent or all powerful. Those things created by such
a God are available to each of us as Soul. All you

TABLE 3

ATTITUDES

1. Awareness of past karmic effects that dominate
    your present life.
2. The five basic passions (lust, greed, anger,
    attachment, vanity) will prevent one from Travel
    by Soul.
3. Remove all fear of the unknown, such as fear of
    things beyond the the physical senses, fear of
    ridicule from the orthodox.
4. Establish a state of consciousness within the
    present moment or in the Now of Time. Why?
5. Accept the responsibility for what you do.
6. Agree to be agreeable to the emotional and
    mental activities of the state of consciousness
    desired.
7. Be open to acceptance.
8. Study all facts with DOUBT in mind. Examine
    everything about a thing; even your reaction to
    it. Ask all kinds of questions ... as a child.
9. Awareness - be concerned with the strength of the
    impressions of effects. Awareness can be both
    mental and spiritual. The effect of the impressions
    sensed by your senses determines your mental
    awareness of it and you need awareness to provide
    understanding. Understanding provides reality of
    the CAUSE which caused it to happen.
10. Hold an attitude of serving God ...
11. Attitude of Love - of the Inner Master, Living
    Spiritual Master.

TABLE 3 (cont.)

CONDITIONS

1. Determine what state of consciousness you want to
    experience. Learn first on physical plane - where
    vibrations are slow. Learn next on Astral plane,
    etc.

2. Learn to place your attention on that state. Mind
    discipline, Need, Urgency.

3. Adjust yourself to the definite set of rules and
    beliefs and knowledge of that state of conscious-
    ness. Rules of shopwork, Rules of sewing, etc.

4. Establish a definite set of goals (specific ones).
    The mind meeds discipline - something to guide it.

TABLE 3 (cont.)

CONDITIONS

5. Change your goal from seeking God (beseeching, prayer, exploitation) to serving God (mastership of your everyday affairs).

6. Learn to serve God as a DOER. If we separate ourselves from God as a Doer, we revert back to become a searcher again, or as a believer again which is passive.

7. Trust in the Heart - which is our word for consciousness.

8. Stand in God's Presence as a beholder, watching God at work. The voice of God has been manifested ... by you !!

TABLE 3 (cont.)

THINGS NEEDED

1. Use the Holograms of Soul:
        To serve God,
        To cleanse our body and Soul.
        To make things happen for God.
        The Holograms of Soul provides this creative
        work.

    The Supreme Deity's message or communications come
    to you:
        as a deep beat,
        as a feeling of warmth,
        as the weight that has fallen from your
          shoulders,
        as that "Ah - Ha feeling" (a job well done),

    God speaks to us through:
        dreams,
        contemplations,
        Daily life experiences.

TABLE 3 (cont.)

THINGS NEEDED

2. Now that you have attained the state of consciousness of your desire,
   Ask as many questions as you need to, to understand all about that thing or object, thought,
   concept, or whatever the consciousness is.
   Remember - You are trying to become self-
   conscious of the state and you want to obtain
   enough self-knowledge of it as you can to
   master it. When you run out of things to ask
   about - your mind will flit off into or onto
   something else.
3. Learn to grasp the knowledge of how to change the
   states within yourself - and yet not change yourself.
4. Travel by Soul is the ability to move from one state
   of consciousness to another state of consciousness;
   all the time one is aware of what one is experiencing
   and is in control of the experience throughout!!

CONCLUSIONS:
   Conscious Awareness - is Knowing.
   Unawareness - is that which we do not know - yet.
   When one reaches the upper worlds - one finds them
   to be the conscious planes of Knowing.

135

have to do is to reach out for it and possess it. It has to be very amazing to realize that you can enter any and all of the states of consciousness created for you simply by doing it!!

Table 3 is a listing of the Attitudes, Conditions, and the Things Needed to enhance your exercise. Contemplate on them.

There are many Blessings waiting for you to enjoy them. Now you can create many, many more blessings of your own. You can make the Blessings Be!

IN CONCLUSION ...

The way the chela produces the forms is the concept of the Holograms of Soul. This is the way I've been told on the inner for me to serve God the Supreme Deity as a coworker with the Supreme Deity during this lifetime. By holding the attitude of serving God, the Holograms of Soul provide the creative work; you can cause the thought form to be manifest on the physical plane.

You stand in God's presence as the beholder, watching God at work. The voice of God has been manifest through you, the channel ... WOW!

Through you, the channel, all things are made and manifested by the Word (Spirit) made flesh. The Light and Sound bring the pure state into Being. These holograms create form of the light to manifest

on the physical. It is understood that to live in
the pure state, we must exist and act in purity. Of
course, the pure state of consciousness is the God
Conscious State, the highest state attainable.
    When one creates the forms of the thoughts of
Soul, one is the channel through which God's pure
state is made flesh.
    By using the Holograms of Soul we replace the
earthly thought forms of mind, cleansing and
purifying us in the process.
    The Sound current and the laser Light of the
Holograms of Soul bring the pure state into Being,
the God Consciousness.

The chela is now THE LIGHT OF THE WORLD!!!
                THE VEHICLE -- THE CHANNEL

The Art
of
TRAVELING BY SOUL
(An Out Of Body Experience)

ORDER FORM

Orders may be placed using money orders, check, or
  bank drafts.
Quantity
_____   The Art of TRAVELING BY SOUL, an Out of
                Body Experience.
$15.00ea   Shipment prepaid.
_____   Total
_____   8.4% Sales Tax (Washington residents only)
                Small orders add $1.00 per book
_____   Final Total (Price includes postage and
                handling)
Please enclose check or international money order
payable in U.S. dollars or fill out credit card
information below.
MAIL MY ORDER TO:
(Please type or print clearly)

Name _____ID# _____

Address _____

City _____State/Prov. _____

Zip/Postal Code _____Country_____
Charge to my VISA___MASTERCARD___EUROCARD___
Card # _____Exp. Date ___Signature _____
MAIL THIS FORM TO:POPULAR PUBLICATIONS, P.O. BOX 1558,
OROVILLE, WASHINGTON 98844, U.S.A.

The Art
of
TRAVELING BY SOUL
(An Out Of Body Experience)

ORDER FORM

Orders may be placed using money orders, check, or bank drafts.

Quantity

_____   The Art of TRAVELING BY SOUL, an Out of Body Experience.

$15.00ea   Shipment prepaid.

_____   Total

_____   8.4% Sales Tax (Washington residents only)
             Small orders add $1.00 per book

_____   Final Total (Price includes postage and handling)

Please enclose check or international money order payable in U.S. dollars or fill out credit card information below.

MAIL MY ORDER TO:

(Please type or print clearly)

Name _____ID# _____

Address _____

City _____State/Prov. _____

Zip/Postal Code _____Country_____

Charge to my VISA___MASTERCARD___EUROCARD___

Card # _____Exp. Date ____Signature _____

MAIL THIS FORM TO:POPULAR PUBLICATIONS, P.O. BOX 1558, OROVILLE, WASHINGTON 98844, U.S.A.